OLD TESTAMENT GUIDES

General Editor
R.N. Whybray

PSALMS

PSALMS

J. Day

Sheffield Academic Press

First published by JSOT Press 1992
Reprinted 1993, 1995, 1996, 1999

Copyright © 1992, 1993, 1995, 1996, 1999 Sheffield Academic Press

Published by
Sheffield Academic Press Ltd
Mansion House
19 Kingfield Road
Sheffield S11 9AS
England

Typeset by Sheffield Academic Press
and
Printed on acid-free paper in Great Britain
by Cromwell Press
Trowbridge, Wiltshire

British Library Cataloguing in Publication Data

A catalogue record for this book is available
from the British Library

ISBN 1-85075-703-8

CONTENTS

PREFACE

I wish to thank Professor R.N. Whybray for the invitation to
write on the Psalms for the 'Old Testament Guides' series, and
for his patience in waiting for the manuscript. I have long felt
the need for an introduction to the Psalms suitable for under-
graduates (and others) which is both comprehensive and
readable, and I trust this work will fulfil that need. I am especially grateful to Professor Whybray for his comments on the
manuscript, and I also wish to thank Dr Susan Gillingham
and Miss Clare Garner (a second year undergraduate) who
kindly commented on earlier drafts. Finally, I must express
my gratitude to Professor David Clines, who read the proofs
with great care and thereby prevented many errors from
entering the text.

John Day
Oxford
October, 1990

N.B. It should be noted that the verse numbers of psalms are
sometimes one higher in the Hebrew text than those given in our
English Bibles. In this volume the verse numbers cited are those of the
English Bible.

ABBREVIATIONS

ANEP	J.B. Pritchard (ed.), *The Ancient Near East in Pictures relating to the Old Testament* (2nd edn with supplement), Princeton: Princeton University Press, 1969
ANET	J.B. Pritchard (ed.), *Ancient Near Eastern Texts relating to the Old Testament* (3rd edn with supplement), Princeton: Princeton University Press, 1969
BJRL	*Bulletin of the John Rylands Library*
BWANT	Beiträge zur Wissenschaft vom Alten und Neuen Testament
BZAW	Beihefte zur Zeitschrift für die alttestamentliche Wissenschaft
CBQ	*Catholic Biblical Quarterly*
FRLANT	Forschungen zur Religion und Literatur des Alten und Neuen Testaments
Gibson	J.C.L. Gibson (ed.), *Canaanite Myths and Legends*, Edinburgh: T. & T. Clark, 1978
JAOS	*Journal of the American Oriental Society*
JBL	*Journal of Biblical Literature*
JSOT	Journal for the Study of the Old Testament (Supplement Series)
JSS	*Journal of Semitic Studies*
JTS	*Journal of Theological Studies*
OTS	*Oudtestamentische Studiën*
RSV	Revised Standard Version
VT	*Vetus Testamentum*
WMANT	Wissenschaftliche Monographien zum Alten und Neuen Testament
ZAW	*Zeitschrift für die alttestamentliche Wissenschaft*

Some Commentaries on the Psalms

A.A. Anderson, *Psalms*, 2 vols. (New Century Bible), London: Oliphants, 1972. (This fine commentary provides a balanced and judicious approach to problems of interpretation.)

P.C. Craigie, *Psalms 1–50* and L.C. Allen, *Psalms 101–150* (Word Biblical Commentary), Waco: Word Books, 1983. (The volume by M.E. Tate on *Psalms 51–100* has not yet appeared, but the two volumes which have been published so far provide a good, useful and up-to-date commentary.)

M.J. Dahood, *Psalms*, 3 vols. (Anchor Bible Commentary), Garden City: Doubleday, 1965-70. (To be used with great care: this is an eccentric commentary which constantly rewrites the Hebrew text on the basis of alleged Ugaritic parallels!)

J.H. Eaton, *Psalms* (Torch Bible Paperbacks), London: SCM, 1967. (Useful brief commentary; it reflects the distinctive view of the author that there are a large number of royal psalms.)

E.S. Gerstenberger, *Psalms, Part 1* (The Forms of Old Testament Literature), Grand Rapids: Eerdmans, 1988. (Part 1 goes up to Ps. 60 and Part 2 has not yet been published. The work, in keeping with the series in which it appears, is dominated by form-critical concerns. It is also pervaded by the author's eccentric views on the late dating and non-temple origin of the psalms.)

H. Gunkel, *Die Psalmen*, Göttingen: Vandenhoeck & Ruprecht, 1926, reprinted 1968 and 1986. (A fine commentary by a scholar whose form-critical analysis of the Psalms is still influential.)

L. Jacquet, *Les Psaumes et le coeur de l'homme*, 3 vols., Gembloux: Duculot, 1975-79. (A large work concentrating on the spiritual themes and Christian interpretation of the psalter.)

H.-J. Kraus, *Psalms*, 2 vols., Minneapolis: Augsburg, 1988-89. (A fine, thorough commentary in the Germanic tradition.)

A.F. Kirkpatrick, *The Book of Psalms* (Cambridge Bible for Schools and Colleges), Cambridge: Cambridge University Press, 1902. (Though inevitably dated in certain respects, this fine old commentary by a careful and judicious scholar still retains considerable value.)

J.W. Rogerson and J.W. McKay, *Psalms,* 3 vols. (Cambridge Bible Commentary), Cambridge: Cambridge University Press, 1977. (Useful brief commentary.)

A. Weiser, *The Psalms* (Old Testament Library), London: SCM, 1962. (A good commentary by a noted German scholar, marked by a tendency to interpret far too many psalms in terms of a Covenant Renewal festival.)

C. Westermann, *The Living Psalms,* Edinburgh: T. & T. Clark, 1990. (Not a full-blown commentary but a work primarily containing an exposition of some fifty selected psalms arranged according to eleven different form-critical categories.)

Some General Books on the Psalms

B.W. Anderson, *Out of the Depths. The Psalms speak for us today,* Philadelphia: Westminster, 1983. (Readable introduction.)

P.D. Miller, *Interpreting the Psalms,* Philadelphia: Fortress, 1986. (An up-to-date and interesting discussion.)

S. Mowinckel, *The Psalms in Israel's Worship,* 2 vols., Oxford: Blackwell, 1962. (A classic work by a master of Psalm study.)

L.J. Sabourin, *The Psalms: Their Origin and Meaning,* 2 vols., Staten Island: The Society of St. Paul, 1969. (An introduction noteworthy for its thorough and comprehensive treatment.)

K. Seybold, *Introducing the Psalms,* Edinburgh: T. & T. Clark, 1990. (A good up-to-date introduction to the Psalms.)

O. Keel, *The Symbolism of the Biblical World: Ancient Near Eastern Iconography and the Book of Psalms,* New York: Seabury, 1978. (This differs from works cited above and has a unique approach, the text and illustrations illuminating the imagery of the psalms from the standpoint of ancient near eastern iconography.)

Some Works on the Psalms in German

H. Gunkel and J. Begrich, *Einleitung in die Psalmen,* 2 vols., Göttingen: Vandenhoeck & Ruprecht, 1928-33. (This classic work, initiated by Gunkel and following his death completed by Begrich, provides a most thorough form-critical analysis of the psalms.)

O. Loretz, *Die Psalmen* 2 (Alter Orient und Altes Testament), Neukirchen-Vluyn: Neukirchener Verlag, 1979. (So far only vol. 2, on Pss. 90–150, of this two-volume work has appeared.) Although arranged in the order of the Psalter, this is not a full-blown commentary. Rather the emphasis falls on the author's distinctive 'textological' approach, analysing lines in terms of numbers of letters. The psalms are dated late.)

S. Mowinckel, *Psalmenstudien,* 6 vols., Kristiania (Oslo): Dybwad, 1921-24. (This classic and pioneering work by a distinguished Norwegian scholar gives a full statement of his early views, and may be compared with his later book, *The Psalms in Israel's Worship.*)

1

INTRODUCTION

The Different Types of Psalm

ANYONE WHO READS through the Psalter will be struck by the variety of compositions which it contains, reflecting diverse moods and situations. At the same time, it is easy to observe that many psalms belong together in distinct groups, as, for example, those centred upon the theme of 'Praise the Lord' (Hallelujah), or those in which a psalmist pours out his distress to God and asks for deliverance. Certain psalms, however, are not so easy to categorize.

Although earlier attempts to categorize the psalms were made in the nineteenth century, most notably by W.M.L. de Wette, it was the work of another German scholar, H. Gunkel, in the earlier part of this century, which proved to be a decisive turning point in analysing the psalms into types. Both in his Psalms commentary and in his *Introduction to the Psalms*, completed after his death by his student J. Begrich, Gunkel strove rigorously to define all the psalms in the Psalter according to their respective types (*Gattungen*) and to discover each type's original life-setting (*Sitz im Leben*). This kind of study is known as form criticism, analysing the biblical literature as it does on the basis of formal or structural criteria.

Gunkel analysed the five main types of psalm as follows:

Hymns. These are psalms of praise. Characteristically they open with a call to praise, follow with the motivation for praising, and conclude with a renewed call for praise. They may extol God for his work in creation or acts in history. Examples are Psalms 33; 117; 145–50. Two sub-categories are the enthronement psalms (Psalms 47; 93; 96–99), which celebrate Yahweh's enthronement as king, and Zion psalms (e.g. Psalms 46; 76; 87), which glory in Mt Zion, Yahweh's holy dwelling place in Jerusalem.

Communal laments. These are psalms in which the nation laments some public disaster that has come upon it, for example the destruction of the Jerusalem temple (Psalms 74; 79) or some other disaster (e.g. Psalms 60; 80; 126). After an opening invocation of God, there is no fixed order in what follows, though the main part of the psalm tends to consist of a complaint directed at God and pleas to him for deliverance.

Royal psalms. These are psalms centring on the king, whom Gunkel understood to be the pre-exilic Israelite monarch. Amongst other things they deal with the king's coronation (Psalms 2; 110), marriage (Psalm 45) and battles (Psalms 18; 20; 144). They are not strictly a form-critical category, since there is no typical structure, but a class delineated purely on grounds of content.

Individual laments. Just as communal laments lament the fate of the nation, so individual laments lament the fate of the particular individual who utters them. They are by far the most common type of psalm in the Psalter, especially the first half, e.g. Psalms 3–7; 22; 25–28; 51; 54–57; 139–143. Characteristically these psalms open with an invocation of Yahweh, they often follow on with the lament proper and pleas for help, and sometimes end on a note of confidence. However, there is no absolute regularity in the ordering or inclusion of particular elements.

As an appendix to the individual laments, Gunkel included the *psalms of confidence* (e.g. Psalms 11; 16; 23). These are psalms in which the psalmist expresses his confidence that God delivers him from evils and enemies, the kind of thing complained about in the individual lament psalms.

Individual thanksgiving psalms. Not so common as the individual laments, these nevertheless form their obverse, since in them the psalmist thanks God for deliverance from personal distress. They include such psalms as Psalms 30; 32; 34; 41; 116; and 138. Again there is no absolute regularity in structure, but they may include an introduction, in which the psalmist declares his intention to thank Yahweh, a narrative section, in which the previous distress is described as well as the prayer for deliverance and its fulfilment, and finally a conclusion.

In addition to these five major types, Gunkel also recognized the existence of a number of other less common types. These include the *communal thanksgiving psalms* (e.g. Psalm 124), a very small category, in which the nation as a whole thanks God for some particular deliverance; the *wisdom psalms*, which are poems of a didatic nature reflecting the influence of the Old Testament wisdom tradition, some more confident of the just working of the world (e.g. Psalms 1; 112) and others more questioning (e.g. Psalms 37; 49); *pilgrimage psalms* (Psalms 84; 122) which were sung by pilgrims on their way to Jerusalem; and *liturgies* (more often called entrance liturgies), in which the worshipper seeking entry to the sanctuary was instructed as to the necessary conditions (Psalms 15; 24), as well as prophetic liturgies in which prophetic oracles were detected (e.g. Psalms 75; 85). Finally, those psalms which could not be assigned to any of the above categories Gunkel called *mixed poems*, which drew on various other forms (e.g. Psalm 119).

In broad terms the main outline of the psalm types as distinguished by Gunkel has been followed by most subsequent scholarship. There have, of course, been disagreements over details, for example whether a psalm should be assigned to this or that category; but this is understandable, since form criticism is not an exact science. The psalm writers were free to compose any psalm they chose, and were not bound by rigid concepts of form, so that the allocation of psalms to particular categories is not always a straightforward business. Gunkel was probably wrong in seeing the psalms of confidence as simply an adjunct to the individual lament psalms, since though they have connections with them, they also have points of contact with the individual thanksgiving psalms, yet belong to neither class and should be seen as a fully distinct genre. Gunkel may also be criticized for inconsistency, in that some of his categories are based on formal or structural criteria (e.g. hymns, thanksgiving and lament psalms) whereas others are established on the basis of content (e.g. royal and wisdom psalms and the sub-categories of hymn known as enthronement and Zion psalms). However, this is probably the price we have to pay for a really useful system of psalm classification: to ignore content completely would not be profitable, and in any case, there is no absolute rigidity of form even in the hymns, laments and thanksgiving psalms.

There have been further quibbles over the terminology for laments and thanksgiving psalms/hymns, as well as over the very existence of communal thanksgiving psalms (see Chapters 2 and 3). Much more radical criticisms of Gunkel's classificatory system have been made by H.-J. Kraus. He proposes that an entirely new system should be constructed based on terms used in the Psalter, especially in the headings. This is not the place to discuss his proposal in detail. Suffice it to say that it is far from satisfactory. For example, his sixth category 'Festival psalms and liturgies' is not based on any terminology used in the Psalter, and his second category 'Songs of Prayer' (*t^epillâ*)—a term used in the headings of Psalms 17; 86; 90; 102; and 142—is employed by Kraus to cover too broad a range of psalms to be useful, including as it does all lament and thanksgiving psalms, whether individual or communal.

In broad terms, therefore, the main outlines of Gunkel's classificatory system may still be followed, though there is always scope for disagreement about details. We shall be examining the various types of psalm in more detail in subsequent chapters.

The Cultic Setting of the Psalms

Both ancient writers and critical scholars of the nineteenth and early twentieth century tended to regard the psalms as providing evidence of private, individual devotion in Israel. Ancient authorities were, of course, bound by the traditional psalm headings; but earlier critical scholars, though rejecting the originality of these superscriptions, were still inclined to see the psalms as individual compositions, reflecting particular historical circumstances. Even Gunkel, who played a significant role in the form-critical analysis of the Psalter, failed to attain a complete cultic understanding of the psalms. While he rightly saw that psalmography must go back to preexilic times and that some of our psalms date from that period, he believed that the majority of our extant psalms are post-exilic 'spiritualized' imitations of the earlier cultic psalms, and that they derived from small, more or less private 'conventicles' of pious laymen. He supposed that the many references to cultic matters in the Psalter were only metaphorical.

As a result of the work of Mowinckel, however, this view is no longer generally accepted. The psalms are littered with cultic allusions, which only make sense if they were used in public worship in the temple in Jerusalem. For example, references to the temple include Pss. 23.6; 26.8; 27.4; 63.2; 96.6 and 122.1, and Psalms 24; 68; 118 and 132 make allusion to cultic processions, while similarly Ps. 48.12 alludes to the perambulation around the walls of Mt Zion. References to sacrifices of various kinds are found, e.g. sacrifices generally (Pss. 4.5; 27.6), burnt offerings (Ps. 20.3), a covenant sacrifice (Ps. 50.5), and a freewill offering (54.6). Mention is also made of dancing (Pss. 30.11; 87.7; 149.3; 150.4), singing (Pss. 9.11; 30.4; 33.2; 47.6-7), and various kinds of musical instrument (Pss. 33.2; 47.5; 81.2; 98.6; 150.5).

Support for the cultic interpretation of the psalms may be found in the Mishnah and other rabbinic sources, which stipulate various cultic occasions for the use of the psalms. Some of the psalm headings also attest liturgical usage, though they also contain some uncertainties. When we come to the late period, we actually find psalms composed in non-cultic, pious circles, specifically the *Psalms of Solomon* and the Qumran *Hodayoth* (Thanksgiving Psalms). These differ markedly from our Old Testament psalms in various ways, and their non-cultic orientation highlights all the more the cultic nature of the biblical psalms.

E.S. Gerstenberger has recently argued that the great majority of the psalms derive not from the Jerusalem temple, but primarily from small-group local community worship, mainly the synagogue of the post-exilic period. However, the grounds for this theory are not convincing. We know nothing about synagogue worship in the Persian period—it is not even certain that synagogues existed then—and Gerstenberger gives insufficient weight to the indications of a temple cult origin as well as to evidence that a very large number of psalms

are pre-exilic. It should also be noted that some scholars who
accept a temple setting for psalms generally make an exception of the wisdom and torah psalms, locating them in a school
context, but even this is somewhat doubtful (see Chapter 4).

As a book of cultic songs the Psalter has sometimes been
referred to in the past as 'the hymn book of the second temple',
i.e. of the post-exilic period. This is fair enough, provided that
we remember that a considerable part of it was also the 'hymn
book' of the first temple, i.e. of the pre-exilic period. We shall be
discussing questions of dating in more detail in subsequent
chapters, but in broad terms one can say that there appears to
be a predominance of pre-exilic psalms in the first two-thirds
of the Psalter and of post-exilic psalms in the last third.
Whereas it was fashionable at the end of the nineteenth and
early part of the twentieth century to regard most psalms as
late (to the extent that B. Duhm could regard the exilic Psalm
137 as the earliest psalm), it later became generally
recognized that there are a large number of pre-exilic psalms
(a trend carried to extremes by I. Engnell who regarded Psalm
137 as the latest). Although in recent years a few scholars
have attempted to argue again that the Psalter is
predominantly post-exilic (e.g. Gerstenberger, O. Loretz), most
would now recognize that there are in fact a large number of
both pre- and post-exilic psalms.

The Psalms and Music

The psalms were composed to be sung to music, as the very
word psalm (Heb. *mizmôr*) indicates. Various types of musical
instrument are mentioned in the Psalter. Among the stringed
instruments were the lyre (Heb. *kinnôr*, e.g. Pss. 33.2; 43.4)
and the harp (Heb. *nēbel* or *nebel*, e.g. Pss. 33.2; 57.8), the latter
being the larger and louder instrument. Wind instruments
included the horn (Heb. *šôpār*, e.g. Pss. 47.5; 98.6), trumpet
(Heb. *ḥªṣōṣªrâ*, Ps. 98.6) and pipe (Heb. *'ûgāb* Ps. 150.4). The
horn, often inaccurately rendered 'trumpet' in the English
Bible, functioned more as a signal than a musical instrument.
Percussion instruments included the cymbals (Heb. *ṣelṣªlîm*,
Ps. 150.4) and a kind of hand drum or tambourine (Heb. *tōp*
[cf. English 'tap'!], e.g. Pss. 149.3; 150.4).

Unfortunately we shall never know what the psalms sounded like when sung to music in ancient Israel. Very little is really known, in fact, about music in the ancient Near East. However, a few years ago a Hurrian psalm from Ugarit in Syria was discovered together with details of its musical notation, dating from the second half of the second millennium BC. A record of the reconstructed Hurrian psalm has been produced, the music being played on a lyre based on ancient patterns. See A.D. Kilmer, R.L. Crocker, and R.R. Brown, *Sounds from Silence: Recent Discoveries in Ancient Near Eastern Music*. Although we cannot know how close this Hurrian psalm music stands to that of ancient Israel, it does at least enable us to catch a glimpse of the cultic music of Israel's environment.

There are a number of obscure musical expressions in the headings to the psalms. Sometimes they may denote a tune, for instance 'According to the lilies' (Psalms 45; 69). Scattered throughout the psalms is the word Selah. The most likely view is that this refers to a musical (instrumental) interlude; this has the support of the Greek Septuagint, which always renders it as *diapsalma* 'musical interlude'. Further support for this view comes from the fact that Selah often comes at the end of a strophe or where there is some natural division or change of mood in the psalm (cf. Pss. 44.8; 46.7, 11; 89.37).

Further Reading

On the different types of psalm (most psalm commentaries discuss this subject in their introductions):

H. Gunkel and J. Begrich, *Einleitung in die Psalmen*.
A.R. Johnson, 'The Psalms', in H.H. Rowley (ed.), *The Old Testament and Modern Study*, Oxford: Clarendon, 1951, 162-209.
S. Mowinckel, *The Psalms in Israel's Worship*.

For a radical alternative to the conventional system of psalm classification see:

H.-J. Kraus, *Psalms* 1, 38–62.

On the cultic setting of the psalms (most psalm commentaries presuppose this viewpoint):

S. Mowinckel, *The Psalms in Israel's Worship*.

Arguing for a non-temple cult origin of the psalms are:

R. Albertz, *Persönliche Frömmigkeit und offizielle Religion* (Calwer theologische Monographien), Stuttgart: Calwer, 1978.

E.S. Gerstenberger, *Psalms*, Part 1.

On music:

J.H. Eaton, 'Music's place in worship: a contribution from the Psalms', *OTS* 23 (1984), 85-107.

A.D. Kilmer, R.L. Crocker, R.R. Brown, *Sounds from Silence: Recent Discoveries in Ancient Near Eastern Music*, Berkeley: Bit Enki publications, 1976.

On musical terms in the psalm headings and elsewhere:

H.-J. Kraus, *The Psalms*, 1, parts of 21–32 (for the usual interpretations)

S. Mowinckel, *The Psalms in Israel's Worship*, 2, parts of 207-17 (offers some speculative cultic interpretations of some of the expressions commonly understood to be musical).

2

PSALMS OF LAMENT

The Individual Lament Psalms

Introduction and Structure

THE INDIVIDUAL LAMENTS have rightly been called the backbone of the Psalter, for they are the commonest type of psalm. Almost one-third of the Psalter belongs to this genre and the following psalms are generally ascribed to it: Psalms 3–7; 9/10; 13; 17; 22; 25–28; 31; 35; 38–39; 40.13-17 = 70; 42/43; 51–52; 54–57; 59; 61; 64; 69–71; 77; 86; 88; 94.16-23; 102; 109; 120; 130; 139–143.

The individual lament psalms do not all conform to one fixed structure. However, almost all of them begin with an invocation of Yahweh, e.g. 'Be gracious to me, O God' (Ps. 56.1). Quite a lot of these psalms follow on next with the lament proper. This may include statements about the distress which the psalmist is suffering, e.g. 'For insolent men have risen against me, ruthless men seek my life; they do not set God before them' (Ps. 54.3) or questions directed at God such as 'How long must I bear pain in my soul, and have sorrow in my heart all the day?' (Ps. 13.2). A few psalms, however, lack a proper lament section (e.g. Psalms 61; 130), though this is always in the background. Sometimes the psalm may include a protestation of innocence, e.g. 'I wash my hands in innocence' (Ps. 26.6) or a confession of sin, e.g. 'For I know my transgressions, and my sin is ever before me' (Ps. 51.3), though often neither is present. Most psalms contain a petition to Yahweh, and this usually follows the lament section, though occasionally it precedes it, as in Psalm 120. The petition characteristically implores Yahweh to deliver the psalmist from his distress, as in Ps.

71.12, 'O God, be not far from me; O my God, make haste to help me!' Sometimes the petition also includes a desire for vengeance on the psalmist's enemies, e.g. 'May my accusers be put to shame and consumed; with scorn and disgrace may they be covered who seek my hurt' (Ps. 71.13). A fair number of individual laments conclude on a positive note, expressing confidence in Yahweh's deliverance, e.g. Ps. 13.5-6, 'But I have trusted in thy steadfast love; my heart shall rejoice in thy salvation. I will sing to the Lord, because he has dealt bountifully with me.' Expressions of confidence may on occasion be expressed earlier in a psalm, e.g. Ps. 31.5.

Some scholars prefer to call the laments complaint psalms, (e.g. Westermann) whereas others see them primarily as pleas for help (e.g. Gerstenberger). C. Broyles, on the other hand, has recently argued that the term complaint psalm should be reserved for those in which Yahweh himself is reproached (e.g. Psalms 6; 35; 39), while those (the majority) in which this is not the case should be called plea psalms (e.g. Psalms 57; 59; 61). The terminology is not wholly felicitous, however, since almost all the lament psalms contain complaints (even if not directly against Yahweh) as well as pleas. Nevertheless, it certainly is the case that there are some psalms, characterized by such expressions as 'How long?' (not merely a plea for information!) which seem to hold Yahweh responsible for the psalmist's distress, whereas many appeal to Yahweh for help without blaming him. As Broyles points out, the individual lament psalms which hold Yahweh responsible tend to be particularly associated with near-death experiences, and the communal lament psalms which hold Yahweh responsible tend to be particularly associated with national disasters in which deliverance seems unduly delayed. It is debatable, however, whether the lament psalms should be divided as neatly into two separate sub-groups as Broyles proposes. For example, Psalms 27; 69 and 143 are called plea psalms by Broyles, but they all contain requests to Yahweh not to hide his face (Pss. 27.9; 69.17; 143.7). There is surely only a fine line between this and some of Broyles' complaint psalms which declare that Yahweh is hiding his face from the psalmist (Pss. 13.1; 88.14). Moreover, Ps. 102.2 also contains the request to Yahweh not to hide his face, but this psalm is regarded by Broyles as a complaint psalm on the basis of vv. 11 and 24, while Pss. 38.1 and 69.26 clearly hold God responsible for suffering but are called plea psalms by Broyles. It is surely better to think of a continuum ranging from psalms in which Yahweh is blamed outright for suffering, through psalms in which he is regarded as passively standing back, to psalms in which God is not explicitly held responsible at all, rather than attempting to divide all the lament psalms neatly into two groups.

The individual lament psalms have been the subject of considerable dispute, especially with regard to the identity of the enemies and the nature of the distress envisaged and the identity of the subject of these psalms. It is to these questions that we must now devote our attention.

Royal Psalms?

We have so far been referring to these psalms as individual laments. In 1888, however, R. Smend argued that the 'I' of these psalms did not denote a single individual but was rather a personification of the nation. That this can be the case is shown by Ps. 129.1, '"Sorely have they afflicted me from my youth", let Israel now say'. However, in 1912 E. Balla argued convincingly that the 'I' of the psalms does denote a single individual, unless there are clear indications otherwise, as in Ps. 129.1. That the 'I' in general is not a personification of the nation is shown, he points out, by a series of personal statements in the laments distinguishing the one who speaks from the other cult members (e.g. Pss. 22.22; 27.10; 69.8; 88.8). Rather, in the overwhelming majority of cases, it is clear that 'I' denotes an individual.

Several scholars, however, have argued that though the 'I' is an individual, he has a representative function, speaking on behalf of the nation. On this view we should think of the 'I' as the king or possibly the army commander, or, in the post-exilic period, the high priest. If this view is correct, the individual lament psalms, or a considerable number of them, would be really communal laments in the 'I' form rather than genuine individual laments.

H. Birkeland devoted a monograph to this subject in 1933 in which he argued that in most of the individual laments the enemies are foreigners; and in 1955, in a later book, he maintained that this is always the case, even in the psalms of illness, which he had previously excluded from this interpretation. On this understanding the subject of the psalms would most naturally be someone speaking in a representative function on behalf of the nation, probably the king. In support of his position Birkeland noted that in some psalms the enemies are specifically identified as foreigners (he cites Psalms 9/10; 42/3; 54; 56; 59); he further noted that in some individual lament psalms there is an awareness of the national plight (e.g. Psalm 94); and he further emphasized that the descriptions of the unnamed enemies in the individual laments resemble the descriptions of the undoubtedly foreign enemies in the royal and communal lament psalms.

Mowinckel, in his later work (cf. *The Psalms in Israel's Worship,* in contrast to his earlier *Psalmenstudien*) was persuaded by Birkeland (who had been Mowinckel's pupil) to see a considerable number of the individual lament psalms as being really communal laments in the 'I' form, though he did not envisage as many as did Birkeland. In this category he included Psalms 3; 5; 7; 9/10–12; 17; 22; 25–28; 31; 34–35; 37; 40; 42/3; 51–52; 54–57; 59; 61; 63–64; 69–71; 77; 86; 90; 94; 102; 109; 130; 141–143. More recently, J.H. Eaton has also reargued the case for seeing many of the individual lament psalms as psalms whose subject is the king speaking on behalf of the nation, the enemies being foreigners, though his position is not as extreme as Birkeland's. He sees the following individual laments as possessing clearly royal content: Psalms 3–4; 7; 9/10; 17; 22; 27–28; 35; 40; 57; 59; 69–71; 94; 140 and 143. As less clear cases he includes Psalms 5; 31; 42/43; 51; 54–56; 77; 86; 102; 109; 139; 141 and 142, though he inclines to see these as royal too. Even more recently another British scholar, S.J.L. Croft, though disagreeing with Eaton in many details, nevertheless still sees a high proportion of the individual laments as royal: Psalms 3; 5–7; 9/10; 13; 17; 22; 26–28; 31; 38; 40; 55–57; 59; 61; 69–71; 94; 108; 139–141; 143.

What are we to say of this? It would certainly appear to be the case that there are occasions where the enemies in the individual laments are represented as foreigners. This is explicitly the case in Psalms 9/10; 56 and 59 (cf. Pss. 9.5, 8, 15, 17, 19; 10.16; 56.7; 59.5, 8). However, Birkeland's statement that the enemies are certainly foreigners in Psalms 42/43 and 54 is unproven, since it is unclear whether the 'ungodly people' in Ps. 43.1 are foreigners, and the reading 'foreigners' (*zārīm*) in Ps. 54.3 may be inferior to the reading 'insolent' (*zēdm*) attested in some Hebrew manuscripts and in the Targum (cf. also Ps. 86.14). At any rate, it is clear that the enemies are at least sometimes foreigners in the individual lament psalms. In such psalms it is perfectly plausible to suppose that the subject is the king or some other representative of the nation. Furthermore, we should always be open to the possibility that the enemies are foreigners in those psalms where they are not explicitly stated to be such. It is also interesting to note that Lamentations 3 is couched in the form of an individual lament and, since it reflects the exilic situation after 586 BC, the enemies there too must be foreigners, specifically the Babylonians who invaded Judah and destroyed the temple. Lamentations 3 makes it natural to suppose that it was not uncommon in ancient Israel for individual laments to be composed with reference to foreign enemies. At the same time, however, it also suggests that the speaker in such psalms need not be the king—as is clearly not the case in Lamentations 3 when there was no longer a king on the throne!

Moreover, one cannot but feel that scholars such as Birkeland, Mowinckel, Eaton and Croft have greatly exaggerated the number of individual lament psalms where the enemies are foreigners and the subject the king. Thus, to begin with, it is clear that Birkeland's claim that the enemies are *always* foreign nations goes beyond the evidence. The fact that there are certain similarities between what is said about enemies in the communal laments and royal psalms, when they are clearly foreigners, and what is said about enemies in the individual laments, should not make us necessarily conclude that the enemies are always foreigners there too, where they are unnamed. It is inevitable that there should be certain features in common between the descriptions of different types of enemy. Furthermore, some of the psalms mentioning enemies are psalms of illness (e.g. Psalms 6; 13; 38; 39; 69; 88), and here it is extremely unnatural to suppose that the enemies are foreigners, as Birkeland eventually came to believe; all the indications are that they are neighbours who have come to despise the psalmist as God-forsaken (cf. also Ps. 41.6ff., an individual thanksgiving psalm for deliverance from illness, where the enemies are even in the bedroom!).

Further arguments against the view that the enemies are primarily foreigners may now be cited, and these are relevant to the views of Mowinckel and Eaton as well as to the more extreme standpoint of Birkeland. Thus, secondly, we find that in the individual lament psalms the psalmist seems to stand alone; there is usually no suggestion that he is representative of a group. (Westermann goes too far, however, when he claims that there is *never* any suggestion of this.) This is most readily explicable if these psalms really are those of ordinary individual Israelites rather than representatives of the nation. Thirdly, it is true that violent and warlike imagery is sometimes attributed to enemies, but there are a number of passages which suggest verbal rather than actual violence. Thus, Ps. 64.3 refers to enemies 'who whet their tongues like swords, who aim bitter words like arrows', and similar expressions are found in Pss. 57.4 and 140.3, 9. As we shall see later, we sometimes may have to do with false and slanderous accusations directed against the psalmist. Fourthly, in a number of psalms it is clear that the enemies are local Israelites, as in Ps. 55.12-14: 'It is not an enemy who taunts me—then I could bear it; it is not an adversary who deals insolently with me—then I could hide from him. But it is you, my equal, my companion, my familiar friend. We used to hold sweet converse together; within God's house we walked in fellowship' (cf. also vv. 20f.). Other examples are Pss. 31.11; 35.11ff.; 69.8, 20f.; 88.8, 18, all four of these psalms being in any case probably psalms of illness (see below).

Fifthly and finally, it is interesting to note that the prophecy of Jeremiah contains a number of passages clearly reflecting the individual lament form (Jer. 11.18–12.6; 15.10-21; 17.14-18; 18.18-23; 20.7-18—Jeremiah's so-called 'confessions'). W. Baumgartner showed convincingly that we should regard Jeremiah as dependent on the psalm form rather than *vice versa*, and this is now generally accepted. The evidence includes such points as the following: the Jeremianic laments show some prophetic influence but the psalms show the pure form, there is other evidence of psalm forms in Jeremiah, and much older individual laments are to be found in the Mesopotamian cult, making it likely that they existed in the Israelite cult before the time of Jeremiah. Accordingly, we have clear evidence from Jeremiah's laments that already in pre-exilic times the individual lament form was used by private citizens and was not confined to the king. Interestingly in Jeremiah we find warlike imagery employed (cf. Jer. 15.20, 'they will fight against you, but they shall not prevail over you'), which, had it occurred in the Psalter, would have led some scholars to insist that real war was being spoken of! This should caution us to be aware of the possibility of the presence of metaphorical language in the description of conflict in the Psalter. (Incidentally, R.P. Carroll's view that the laments in Jeremiah are really communal laments of the exiles is quite unjustified, since throughout the 'I', not the 'we', form is used, and as we have seen in the Psalter, this points to an individual as the subject unless there is strong evidence to the contrary.)

Psalms of Those Who Are Seriously Ill

There is no doubt that some of the individual lament psalms are concerned with illness, though there is some dispute about the precise number of such psalms. Gunkel saw a considerable number of such psalms in the Psalter, and so also did the early Mowinckel. What might seem strange at first sight to the modern reader is the fact that quite often the psalms which complain about illness also complain about enemies (cf. Psalms 6; 13; 38; 39; 69; 88). Gunkel regarded the hostility of the enemies as due to their interpreting the illness as a sign of the guilt and God-forsakenness of the sufferer. This view is certainly the most natural way of understanding these psalms, and it is interesting that we find precisely the same thing in the book of Job, where Job's so-called 'comforters' regard his illness as a sign of his sin (cf. also Job 19.13-22). The only difference is that the psalmists sometimes admit their sin (cf. Pss. 38.3ff.; 39.8, 11), whereas Job maintains his righteousness.

In vol. 1 of his *Psalmenstudien* (1921), however, Mowinckel offered a new explanation. He claimed that the enemies in these psalms are to be understood as sorcerers, who have cast spells on the psalmist, so that the psalms in question are, so to speak, counter-spells. Such is the case with many of the Babylonian psalms. Sometimes in the biblical psalms the enemies are called 'workers of evil' (*pō°lê 'āwen*), as for example in Pss. 5.5; 6.8; 59.2; 64.2; and Mowinckel claimed that this expression refers specifically to sorcerers, the word *'āwen* being a technical term for sorcery.

In general, Mowinckel has had little following in his view. The main points to be brought against Mowinckel are as follows. First, as Gunkel had already pointed out and as has frequently been noted since, there is nothing in the psalms to suggest that the enemies were themselves thought of as being responsible for the illness. Secondly, it is very dubious that the basic meaning of *'āwen* is 'sorcery' and, indeed, there is no instance in the Old Testament where this is the most natural meaning. Thirdly, Hebrew has a root *kšp* referring to sorcery, yet this nowhere occurs in the psalms. Fourthly, it is Yahweh himself who seems to be thought of in these psalms as responsible for the illness (e.g. Pss. 38.1f.; 39.10f.), which makes it unlikely that sorcerers or demons are thought of as the source (though there may be traces of the demonic idea in Psalm 91). Mowinckel himself modified his own view and, without denying that 'the workers of evil' could be sorcerers, came to see the enemies as more often foreigners, a view which we have examined above.

How many individual laments are psalms of illness? As mentioned above, Gunkel and the early Mowinckel saw a considerable number. More recently, K. Seybold has devoted a whole monograph to the illness psalms and has produced carefully worked-out criteria for distinguishing such psalms, primarily on the basis of the particular terminology employed. Of the individual lament psalms, he concludes that Psalms 38 and 88 are certainly illness psalms and Psalms 6, 13 and 51 are probably such, while there is a distinct possibility that this is also the case with Psalms 31; 35 and 71. Vocabulary suggestive of illness includes such expressions as 'your stroke/plague'

(Ps. 39.10), 'my stroke/plague' (Ps. 38.11) and 'my pain' (Pss. 38.17; 39.2). Seybold's conclusions seem eminently reasonable.

Whereas there is no doubt that the psalms of thanksgiving for deliverance from illness (see below) were sung in the temple by the man who had recovered from his illness, there is uncertainty whether the illness psalms of lament were recited in the cult by the sick person in question. Seybold maintains that the sick person would not have been in a position to do so and that these psalms would rather have been recited at home, though he thinks a representative of the sick man may have recited a psalm in the cult.

Finally, it is interesting to note that some of the psalms of illness employ the imagery of Sheol (the underworld) in describing the condition of the sick man. For example, Ps. 88.3ff. declare:

> For my soul is full of troubles, and my life draws near to Sheol. I am reckoned among those who go down to the Pit; I am a man who has no strength, like one forsaken among the dead, like the slain that lie in the grave, like those whom thou dost remember no more, for they are cut off from thy hand. Thou hast put me in the depths of the Pit, in the regions dark and deep.

Note that the sick man is already reckoned as being in Sheol: this reflects what has often been said of the Hebrews, that for them illness was itself a sign of the intrusion of Sheol into life, a kind of death.

Psalms of Those Who Have Been Unjustly Accused

It has been argued, especially by some German scholars, that some of the individual laments are pleas for vindication on the part of persons against whom false or unjust accusations have been made.

There are several variations on this general approach. It was H. Schmidt who first elaborated this kind of interpretation. He held that many of the individual laments (Psalms 3–5; 7; 11; 13, 17; 25–27; 31; 35; 38–39; 41–42/43; 52; 54–59; 69; 77; 86; 88; 94; 102; 109; 139–140; 142) had their setting in a sacral trial during which the accused was held under detention in the temple. One can see that at least some of the psalms make sense as the pleas of those who have been falsely accused.

Thus, for example, Ps. 27.12 declares that 'false witnesses have risen against me', and similarly we read in v. 2 that 'evildoers assail me, uttering slanders against me'. Again, Psalm 26 sounds like a plea for vindication in the face of false accusations, for it opens with the words 'Vindicate me, O Lord, for I have walked in my integrity', and continues in v. 6 with the psalmist saying, 'I wash my hands in innocence'. Ps. 7.3ff. too sounds like an avowal of innocence in the face of slanderous accusations: 'O Lord my God, if I have done this, if there is wrong in my hands, if I have requited my friend with evil or plundered my enemy without cause, let the enemy pursue me and overtake me, and let him trample my life to the ground, and lay my soul in the dust'. However, it is surely wrong to see the vast number of psalms cited by Schmidt as having their setting in this context. Many of the individual lament psalms lack any indications which would enable one to posit so precise a context. Moreover, there is nothing in them to indicate that the psalmist was undergoing detention in the temple, and the passages outside the psalter to which Schmidt appeals for evidence of sacral trial (Exod. 22.7f.; Deut. 17.7; 1 Kgs 8.31f.) say nothing of detention.

Another scholar, W. Beyerlin, shares the view that in a number of individual lament psalms the psalmist is undergoing a sacral trial in the temple. The one falsely accused utters a psalm in order to encourage Yahweh to intervene in judgment in his favour. This judgment is understood as taking place in the cult. Beyerlin does not think that all the individual lament psalms have this particular institutional background, but he maintains that Psalms 3; 4; 5; 7; 11; 17; 23; 26; 27; 57 and 63 do. His position is clearly more modest than Schmidt's, since he does not postulate cultic detention, for which there is no evidence, and the number of psalms which he brings into connection with his proposed cultic trials is far fewer. Some psalms (e.g. Psalms 7; 26; 27) certainly do make sense as the pleas of those who have been falsely accused. However, there seems insufficient evidence for postulating anything as formal as a cultic trial even on the lines presented by Beyerlin.

L. Delekat proposed that the individual laments were originally inscriptions left in the temple by those seeking asylum, rather than liturgical compositions, and he seeks to extract much autobiographical information from them. However, Delekat's highly original reconstruction has been widely criticized. It has been rightly pointed out that the Old Testament elsewhere only recognizes the right of asylum to someone slaying another unintentionally (Exod. 21.12-14; Num. 35.9-34; Deut. 19.1-13; Josh. 20), whereas these allegedly asylum psalms never refer to such a person. On the other hand, Delekat proposes on the basis of these psalms the existence of a right of asylum for various other types of person concerning which the Old Testament elsewhere is completely silent. Moreover, nothing in these psalms suggests that they are inscriptions rather than liturgical pieces like other psalms, and Delekat's attempts to find detailed information about these psalmists seems out of place when we recall the very generalized, stereotyped language which the psalms tend to use.

In conclusion, then, it may be stated that none of the detailed proposals of Schmidt, Beyerlin, or Delekat can be accepted. We simply lack the evidence to set the individual lament psalms against the institutional backgrounds that they propose. Nevertheless, it remains entirely plausible that at least some psalms (e.g. Psalms 7; 26; 27) are to be understood as the pleas for vindication of those who have been the subject of unjust accusations.

Other Settings and General Conclusions

Our discussion has shown that there is no single solution to the problem of the speaker of the individual laments or the nature of the enemies referred to. Some psalms may be royal psalms with the enemies being foreign nations; there is, however, far clearer evidence for psalms of illness, with the enemies as the sick person's tormentors, while other psalms seem to reflect a situation of false accusations.

It is necessary, however, to point out that many of the individual laments are phrased in such general, stereotyped terms that it is no longer possible to deduce exactly what the complaint is. This is just what we should expect of psalms that were constantly being used in the liturgy by a variety of people. Many of the individual lament psalms are couched in such vague and general terms that they were probably capable of being employed in a wide range of types of distress. Thus, in addition to three settings that have noted above (conflict with foreign nations, illness and false accusations) one could envisage such situations as persecution (cf. Jeremiah's laments), social oppression (cf. the references to the psalmists as 'poor'), and even general criminality (cf. the similar language in Prov. 1). One clearly cannot seek detailed autobiographical information in these psalms, since they represent general and repeatable rather than once-for-all and particular situations.

The Certainty of a Hearing

In a considerable number of individual lament psalms there occurs a marked change of mood toward the end, with the psalmist expressing confidence that Yahweh has heard his prayer. One may find this in Pss. 6.8ff.; 7.10f.; 13.5f.; 28.6ff.; 31.19ff.; 52.8f.; 55.23; 56.9ff.; 57.7ff.; 61.5; 94.22f.; 130.7f.; and 140.12f. (cf. Jer. 20.11).

Various explanations of this phenomenon have been put forward. Weiser supposed that *sometimes* the psalms are really thanksgiving psalms, in which the lament is recapitulated. However, although there are undoubted individual thanksgiving psalms where this is so (cf. Pss. 30.8-10; 116.3f., 10f.), this is explicitly stated, and the lament forms only a small part of the psalm, whereas in the psalms with which we are here concerned, the laments form by far the largest part of the psalms, so that they are most naturally understood as lament psalms.

A widely followed view is that we should suppose that a priest delivered a salvation oracle in the period between the end of the lament and the beginning of the words implying the 'certainty of hearing', which would then serve as a response to Yahweh's promise of salvation. This theory was first put forward by F. Küchler in 1918. However, it was J. Begrich's article in 1934 which made the most influential contribution to the discussion. He drew attention to the fact that there are a number of 'salvation oracles' in the prophecy of Deutero-Isaiah (Isa. 41.8-13, 14-16; 43.1-3a, 5; 44.2-5; 48.17-19; 49.7, 15f.; 51.7f.; 54.4-8). Characteristic of these oracles are the words 'Fear not, for... ' Begrich noted that some of the expressions found correspond to those used in the individual laments, e.g. Israel is described as a worm both in Ps. 22.6 and Isa. 41.14. He argued that this provided evidence for the existence of a priestly salvation oracle, on which Deutero-Isaiah would have modelled his own oracles delivered to despondent Israel. Turning to the individual lament psalms themselves, Begrich also claimed to find support for the existence of a salvation oracle in Ps. 35.3, where the psalmist cries, 'Say to my soul, "I am your deliverance"', and in Lam. 3.55-57, where we read, 'I called on thy name, O Lord, from the depths of the pit; thou didst hear my plea, "Do not close thine ear to my cry for help!" Thou didst come near when I called on thee; thou didst say, "Do not fear!"' Since Begrich's time ancient near eastern comparative material has also been called in to support the notion of a salvation oracle.

However, a number of scholars have remained unconvinced that the intervention of a priestly salvation oracle should be invoked in order to explain the change of mood at the end of some individual lament psalms. Their strongest argument is that in none of these psalms is the 'certainty of a hearing' preceded by a salvation oracle. This is surprising, since if the divine oracle had intervened at this point, it would surely have been the most important element in the proceedings. Although it might be argued that our psalm texts only give us the words of the psalmist and not the divine response, it is odd that this should have been done with such thoroughgoing consistency, especially when we recall that divine oracles are not unknown elsewhere in the Psalter (cf. Ps. 60.6-8 = 108.8-10) and that the individual laments are so numerous. It ought also to be noted that expressions of confidence are sometimes found in individual laments elsewhere than at the end: if a salvation oracle is not necessary to explain this phenomenon, need it be invoked to explain expressions of confidence when they come at the end? The fact that such sentiments are more frequent at the end of psalms is entirely understandable: the psalmist would want to end on a positive note and such feelings would have been encouraged by the very act of praying (see below). The point has also been made (by A. Szörényi) that if the changes of mood are to be attributed to the intervention of a priestly salvation oracle, it is odd that we never have psalms ending on a note that might imply the intervention of a priestly response of judgment—did the priests always proclaim salvation? It is possible to argue that Deutero-Isaiah's salvation oracles may have been taken over from some other context than the ordinary individual lament; E. Conrad, for instance, has recently argued that they are appropriated from divine oracles delivered to the king in a war context, which is the case in the ancient near eastern parallels that have been cited.

Conceivably, if there was a priestly salvation oracle, it might have been delivered after the lament psalm was over, including the words expressing confidence in a hearing. It might be this that Ps. 35.3 and Lam. 3.55-57 refer to, though even these passages need not necessarily imply a literal oracle delivered through a priest. If this were the case it would be understandable why the salvation (or judgment) oracles are never preserved, since they would have belonged to a later stage in the proceedings.

Although the theory of a priestly salvation oracle to explain the change of mood at the end of some individual lament psalms is not impossible, the absence of such oracles from the text of our Psalter makes it seriously open to question. It is more likely that the change of mood is to be explained by some inner psychological process in which the psalmist was able to look forward, anticipating the desired deliverance. This explanation gains support from the fact observed by students of prayer that it is not uncommon for those who pray to find that feelings of doubt and despair eventually give rise to feelings of confidence and assurance. As F. Heiler noted in his famous book on *Prayer*, 'A wonderful metamorphosis takes place in the prayer itself, unconsciously, involuntarily, or quite suddenly... ; the feeling of uncertainty and instability is replaced by the blissful consciousness of being cared for, hidden in the hand of a protecting higher Power' (pp. 259-60). In any case it would doubtless have been thought desirable to end on a positive note.

The Communal Lament Psalms

The Communal Laments and their Cultic Setting

One of the major psalm types is that of the communal laments, i.e. psalms in which the nation of Israel as a whole laments its fate before Yahweh and prays that he will deliver them. The psalms commonly attributed to this genre are Pss. 12; 44; 60; 74; 79; 80; 83; 85; 94.1-11; 126 and 137. Psalms 58 and 90 also have some of the characteristics of the communal laments. It will be noted that in number they are far fewer than the individual laments. Outside the Psalter one may note communal laments such as Isa. 63.7–64.11; Jer. 14.2-9, 19-22; Lamentations 5. The communal lament psalms tend to be concerned with political and military disasters which afflict the nation. We have indications from two prophetic texts, Jeremiah 14 and Joel 1–2, that collective lamentation could also be occasioned by other disasters such as drought and locusts.

The *Sitz im Leben* of such psalms is generally accepted to have been special days set aside for lamentation in the temple. We read about such occasions in texts like Josh. 7.5-9; Judg. 20.23, 26; 1 Sam. 7.6; 2 Chron. 20.3ff.; Jeremiah 14; Joel 1–2; Zech. 7.3, 5; 8.19; Judith 4.9-15. Fasting, wearing of sackcloth, weeping, rending of garments, and the putting of dust and ashes on the head were among the actions that took place on such occasions. There is a particularly vivid account of such a ceremony in Judith 4.9-15.

Zech. 7.3, 5 and 8.19 allude to a number of fast days that had been observed during the exile and early post-exilic periods, which commemorated the various disasters that overtook the kingdom of Judah in its final days. One of these, the fast in the fifth month, lamented the burning of the temple in 586 BC, and this event is variously dated to the 7th day of the 5th month (2 Kgs 25.8-9) and the 10th day of the 5th month (Jer. 52.12-13). One can well imagine that psalms such as 74 and 79 were recited on this occasion.

The Structure of the Communal Lament Psalms

The communal laments characteristically open with an invocation of God. There is no fixed order in what follows, but the main part of the lament usually consists of a complaint directly addressed to God and pleas to him for deliverance. The complaint is sometimes in the form of a question, e.g. 'How long... ?' (cf. Pss. 74.10; 79.5; 80.4; 94.3) or 'Why...?' (cf. Pss. 44.24; 74.1, 11) and sometimes in the form of a statement that God has forsaken them or the like (cf. Pss. 44.9-16; 60.1-3; 80.5-6). The plea for deliverance is usually in the imperative form, e.g. 'Rouse thyself... Awake' (Ps. 44.23), 'Arise' (Ps. 74.22), 'Help' (Ps. 12.1), 'Help us' (Ps. 79.9), 'Restore us' (Pss. 80.3, 7, 9; 85.4), 'Restore our fortunes' (Ps. 126.4), or 'protect us, guard us' (Ps. 12.7), though we also find the jussive form used ('let... ', 'may... '), as in Ps. 126.5, 'May those who sow in tears reap with shouts of joy!' The plea for deliverance sometimes involves an imprecation on the enemy (especially harsh in Pss. 137.7-9 and 79.12). The main part of the psalm also tends to contain accusations in the third person plural of what the enemy has done (cf. Pss. 12.1-2, 8; 58.1-5; 74.3b-8; 79.1-3; 80.16; 83.2-8; 94.4-7) and, less frequently, statements about the people's lot in the first person plural (Pss. 44.22; 74.9; 79.4; and especially 137.1-4).

Sometimes Yahweh's gracious acts in the past are cited as a motivation for him to act in the present (cf. Pss. 74.12-17; 80.8-11; 83.9-12; 85.1-3; and possibly 126.1-3) and occasionally there are expressions of innocence (Ps. 44.17-21) or an admission of sin (Ps. 79.8-9). Also, there is occasionally a divine oracle expressing salvation for the people (Pss. 12.5; 60.6-8 = 108.7-9; 85.8-13), an expression of confidence (Ps. 60.12 = 108.13) or a vow of future thanks or obedience (Pss. 79.12; 80.18a).

Dating

Because the communal laments tend to deal with important political disasters, we are in a better position with regard to dating a number of them than with many other psalms. Thus, Psalms 74, 79 and 137 reflect the period of the Babylonian exile following the destruction of the temple in 586 BC. Psalm 137 could not be clearer, with its famous opening lines 'By the rivers of Babylon, there we sat down and wept, when we remembered Zion' and its closing imprecation against the

Babylonians and Edomites because of the 'day of Jerusalem'. Although Psalms 74 and 79 have sometimes been connected with the period of the Maccabean struggle in the second century BC, it is preferable to relate them to the destruction of the temple by the Babylonians in 586 BC. Thus Psalm 74 speaks of the destruction of the temple (v. 7), which fits the events of 586 BC but not Antiochus IV Epiphanes' desecration of the temple in 168 BC, since he only burned the doors of the temple (1 Macc. 4.38; 2 Macc. 1.8) and desecrated the sanctuary (1 Macc. 1.23, 39; 2 Macc. 6.5). Ps. 79.1 hints at the destruction of the temple without stating it explicitly—cf. the parallelism of v. 1, 'they have defiled thy holy temple; they have laid Jerusalem in ruins'—and the psalm makes no reference to a proscription of Judaism such as occurred under Antiochus IV Epiphanes.

Psalm 126 equally clearly refers to the period in the sixth century BC, after Cyrus king of Persia had allowed the Jews to return to Palestine from exile but when the initial optimistic expectations raised by Deutero-Isaiah had not been realized (cf. Hag. 1). This situation explains the contrast between vv. 1ff. and 4ff., 'When the Lord restored the fortunes of Zion, we were like those who dream... Restore our fortunes, O Lord, like the watercourses of the Negeb!' This interpretation seems preferable to the explanation of W. Beyerlin, who believes that the psalm is exilic and that the two parts do not refer to different historical situations, but that the tension is 'between the salvation already apprehended in faith and the plea that it might "appear"'. Beyerlin accordingly renders v. 1 as 'When the Lord restored the fortunes of Zion,—we are like those who dream—'. Another psalm which very plausibly reflects the same period is Psalm 85, for here again we find the same tension between Yahweh's restoration of the nation and renewed lamentation.

Psalm 80 is sometimes thought to be in origin a psalm from the northern kingdom, dating not long before its fall to the Assyrians in 722 BC—note the allusion to the tribes of Ephraim, Benjamin and Manasseh in v. 2. However, the reference to Yahweh enthroned on the cherubim in v. 1 may indicate that it originated in the Jerusalem temple, since the cherubim (winged sphinxes) in the temple constituted Yah-

weh's earthly throne in the viewpoint of the southern kingdom of Judah. A southern origin may also be indicated by v. 11,
if, as seems likely, this looks back nostalgically to the Davidic–
Solomonic empire. The psalm may thus reflect concern for the
north in the south, whether at the end of the eighth or some-
time during the seventh century BC. Interestingly the Septuagint judged the purport of the psalm correctly with its heading 'concerning the Assyrian'.

Psalm 44 clearly reflects a major national military disaster
of some kind, but it is not possible to discern precisely what this
was. The other communal laments are also hard to place precisely.

Further Reading

On the Individual Laments:

G.W. Anderson, 'Enemies and Evildoers in the Book of Psalms',
BJRL 48 (1965), 18-29.

W.H. Bellinger, *Psalmody and Prophecy* (JSOT Supplement
Series, 27), Sheffield: JSOT, 1984.

H. Birkeland, *The Evildoers in the Book of Psalms*, Oslo: Dybwad, 1955.

C.C. Broyles, *The Conflict of Faith and Experience in the
Psalms: a Form-Critical Theological Study* (JSOT Supplement Series, 52), Sheffield: JSOT, 1989.

S.J.L. Croft, *The Identity of the Individual in the Psalms* (JSOT
Supplement Series, 44), Sheffield: JSOT, 1987.

J.H. Eaton, *Kingship and the Psalms*, 2nd edn, Sheffield: JSOT,
1986.

E.A. Leslie, *The Psalms*, New York/Nashville: Abingdon–
Cokesbury Press, 1949. (Contains an exposition of H.
Schmidt's views in English.)

S. Mowinckel, *The Psalms in Israel's Worship* 1, 225-46; and 2,
1-25.

C. Westermann, *Praise and Lament in the Psalms*, Edinburgh:
T. & T. Clark, 1981.

A number of important works on the Individual Laments are in German:

E. Balla, *Das Ich der Psalmen*, Göttingen: Vandenhoeck &
Ruprecht, 1912.

W. Beyerlin, *Die Rettung der Bedrängten in den Feindpsalmen
der Einzelnen auf institutionelle Zusammenhänge unter-*

sucht (FRLANT, 99), Göttingen: Vandenhoeck & Ruprecht, 1970.

H. Birkeland, *Die Feinde des Individuums in der israelitischen Psalmenliteratur*, Oslo: Grøndahl, 1933.

L. Delekat, *Asylie und Schutzorakel am Zionheiligtum*, Leiden: Brill, 1967.

E. Gerstenberger, *Der bittende Mensch*, Neukirchen: Neukirchener Verlag, 1980.

S. Mowinckel, *Psalmenstudien*, 1.

H. Schmidt, *Das Gebet der Angeklagten im Alten Testament* (BZAW, 49), Giessen: A. Töpelmann, 1928.

K. Seybold, *Das Gebet des Kranken im Alten Testament* (BWANT, 99), Stuttgart: W. Kohlhammer. 1973.

On the certainty of a hearing:

J. Begrich, 'Das priesterliche Heilsorakel', *ZAW* 52 (1934), 81-92.

E.W. Conrad, *Fear Not Warrior: A Study of 'al tīrā' Pericopes in the Hebrew Scriptures* (Brown Judaic Studies, 75), Chico: Scholars, 1985.

S.B. Frost, 'Asseveration by Thanksgiving', *VT* 8 (1958), 380-90.

H. Gunkel and J. Begrich, *Einleitung in die Psalmen*, 243-47.

F. Küchler, 'Das priesterliche Orakel in Israel und Juda', in W. Frankenberg and F. Küchler (eds.), *Abhandlungen zur semitischen Religionsgeschichte* (W.W. Graf von Baudissin Festschrift, BZAW, 33), Giessen: A. Töpelmann, 1918, 285-301.

A. Szörényi, *Psalmen und Kult im Alten Testament*, Budapest: Sankt Stefans Gesellschaft, 1961, 286-307.

J.W. Wevers, 'A Study in the Form Criticism of Individual Complaint Psalms', *VT* 6 (1956), 80-96.

On the Individual Laments and Jeremiah's 'Confessions':

W. Baumgartner, *Jeremiah's Poems of Lament*, Sheffield: Almond, 1988.

R.P. Carroll, *From Chaos to Covenant*, London: SCM, 1981, 107-35.

On the Communal Laments generally:

E. Lipiński, *La liturgie pénitentielle dans la Bible* (Lectio Divina, 52), Paris: Les éditions du Cerf, 1969.

S. Mowinckel, *The Psalms in Israel's Worship*, 1, 193-224.

L. Sabourin, *The Psalms: Their Origin and Meaning*, 2, 141-84.

On specific Communal Lament Psalms:

W. Beyerlin, *We are like Dreamers. Studies in Psalm 126*, Edinburgh: T. & T. Clark, 1982.

B. Hartberger, *'An den Wassern von Babylon...' Psalm 137 auf dem Hintergrund von Jeremia 51, der biblischen Edom-Traditionen und babylonischen Originalquellen* (Bonner biblische Beiträge, 63), Frankfurt am Main/Bonn: Peter Hanstein, 1986.

3

PSALMS OF PRAISE AND THANKSGIVING

Hymns

Basic Structure

ONE OF THE MAIN TYPES of psalm is the hymn or psalm of praise (Heb. *t^ehillâ*). Although not all of them have the same structure, a fair number have the following threefold form:

1. Introduced call to praise.

2. The main part of the psalm: motivation for the praise (often introduced by *kî*, 'for').

3. Final repetition of the call to praise.

The shortest psalm in the Psalter, Psalm 117, illustrates this simple structure in the briefest possible way:

1. Praise the Lord, all nations!
   Extol him, all peoples!

2a-b. For great is his steadfast love toward us;
   and the faithfulness of the Lord endures for ever.

2c. Praise the Lord!

There are many variations on this basic form. For example, in addition to 'Praise the Lord', the introductory call to praise can include the words 'Bless the Lord' (Psalm 134), 'Shout to the Lord' (Psalm 100), or 'Rejoice in the Lord' (Psalm 33). Sometimes the introductory call to praise is repeated later in the psalm (Pss. 147.7, 12; 148.7), or it may be omitted altogether, as in the Zion psalms (Psalms 46; 48; 76; 84; 87; 122). F. Crüsemann has argued that in section 2 of the basic structure outlined above, the word *kî*, 'for', is not to be understood as introducing a motivation for praise but rather the contents of the praise. However, it has to be stated that this understanding of *kî* would run counter to normal Hebrew usage. The motivation section may also be introduced in other ways, e.g. by means of participles (Pss. 136.4ff.; 147.8f., 14-17). In Psalm 150 the motivation (v. 2) is almost lost in the midst of the repeated call to praise. The final repetition of the call to praise, which normally concludes the hymns, may also be omitted, as in Psalms 29 and 33.

Various Types of Hymn and their Themes

The hymns include Psalms 8; 19A (i.e. vv. 1-6); 29; 33; 46–48; 65; 66A; 68; 76; 84; 87; 93; 95–100; 103–104 (105); 111; 113–114; 117; 122; 134–36 and 145–50. As will be observed, they are often grouped together and predominate more in the second half of the Psalter, just as laments are more frequently found in the first half. The climactic note of the Psalter is therefore one of praise, and in fact the general title for the Psalter in Hebrew is *t^ehillîm* (lit. 'praises'). Virtually all the hymns in the last third of the Psalter are post-exilic (though very probably not Psalm 104), while many (though not all) in the first two-thirds of the Psalter are pre-exilic.

In the call to praise Yahweh, not only is Israel included, but also foreign nations may be—and, indeed, the whole earth (Pss. 33.8; 47.1; 66.1, 8; 96.1; 97.1; 98.4; 100.1; 145.21; 148.11), the gods or angels (Pss. 29.1; 97.7; 148.2), and even the world of nature (Pss. 19.1-4; 96.11-12; 98.7-8; 148.3-11). Psalm 148 lists a whole catalogue of items (mostly from nature) which are exhorted to praise Yahweh, and it has been suggested by G. von Rad that this reflects the influence of ancient near eastern list wisdom or onomastica, where various items in the universe were listed in encyclopaedic fashion. It has, however, been pointed out more recently by D.R. Hillers that this hypothesis is unnecessary, since Egyptian and Mesopotamian hymns themselves contain lists comparable to Psalm 148; moreover, the onomastica are not in fact particularly close to these psalmic catalogues.

Various reasons are given in the motivation clauses for praising Yahweh. Basically they relate to Yahweh's greatness and goodness as manifested on two main fronts: his creation of the world and his gracious acts in the history of Israel. The former is found, for instance, in Pss. 33.6-9; 65.6-13; 95.4-5; 135.6-7; 136.5-9; 146.6; 147.4, 8-9, 16-18; 148.5-6; and the latter in Pss. 68.7ff.; 135.8-12; 136.10-24 and 147.2. As will be observed, sometimes both themes appear in the same psalm.

Occasionally, a whole psalm centres on the theme of creation or Yahweh's lordship over nature. This is the case in Psalms 8; 19A; 29 and 104. Psalm 8 stands apart from the others in that its thought centres on Yahweh's creation of humanity as distinct from his creation of the world. There are some clear parallels to Gen. 1.26ff., namely the theme of human lordship over the creatures on earth and the comparison of humans with the angels or gods, Yahweh's heavenly court. With regard to the latter, Ps. 8.5 declares that humanity is made 'little less than the gods/angels' (not 'than God'), while in Gen. 1.26ff. humanity is made in their image (this is the point of the phrase 'Let *us* make man in *our* image'). The fact that Psalm 8 is a hymn centring on human beings creates a problem for the thesis of R. Albertz, who argues that whereas the theme of the creation of the world had its original setting in the hymn, that of the creation of man had its original setting in the individual lament. Albertz has to argue that Psalm 8 is a development of the lament, which is unnatural.

Psalm 104 is remarkable not only for the length of its concentration on the subject of creation and its striking parallels with the Egyptian hymn to Aton by Pharaoh Akhenaten (on which see below), but also for the way that the order in topics are treated agrees with the order of creation in Genesis 1:

Ps. 104.1-4	Creation of heaven and earth	Cf. Gen. 1.1-5
Ps. 104.5-9	Waters pushed back	Cf. Gen. 1.6-10
Ps. 104.10-13	Waters put to beneficial use	Implicit in Gen. 1.6-10
Ps. 104.14-18	Creation of vegetation	Cf. Gen. 1.11-12
Ps. 104.19-23	Creation of luminaries	Cf. Gen. 1.14-18
Ps. 104.24-26	Creation of sea creatures	Cf. Gen. 1.20-22
Ps. 104.27-30	Creation of living creatures	Cf. Gen. 1.24-31

Although it has sometimes been supposed that Psalm 104 is dependent on Genesis 1, the reverse is in fact far more likely.

In favour of the priority of the psalm, for example, is the fact that Yahweh's conflict with the chaos waters in Ps. 104.5-9 reflects a more primitive and mythological understanding than Gen. 1.6-10, where God's control of the waters has become essentially a 'job of work'. Similarly, Ps. 104.26 employs the mythological name Leviathan for a sea creature, whereas the corresponding passage in Gen. 1.21 speaks less mythologically of 'great sea monsters'. Again, Gen. 1.24 uses an unusual form of the word for 'beast(s)' ($hay^etô$), which is attested elsewhere only in poetry, including Ps. 104.11, 20, suggesting the dependence of Genesis 1 on some poetic text, presumably Psalm 104.

Striking ancient near eastern parallels can be adduced for three of the hymns centring on Yahweh's power over nature and creation (Psalms 19; 29; 104). Regarding Psalm 104, the parallels with the pharaoh Akhenaten's hymn to the sun (*ANET*, 369-71) are such as to suggest some kind of dependence. The so-called heretic pharaoh undertook a monotheistic revolution and worshipped only the sun disc, Aton, in the fourteenth century BC. Akhenaten's religious revolution did not survive long after his death and it is difficult to know exactly how his hymn came to be known to the author of Psalm 104; but that there is some ultimate connection is clear enough. Interestingly, echoes of Akhenaten's hymn are found much later still in the tomb of Petosiris in Egypt. The parallels are particularly strong with Ps. 104.20-30, where every verse except v. 28 has an equivalent (though not in the same order).

When we come to Psalm 29, the background is Canaanite rather than Egyptian. The sevenfold thunder of the deity (vv. 3-9) combined with his victory over the chaos waters (vv. 3, 10) and exaltation as king (v. 11) is very reminiscent of the Canaanite storm-god Baal, whose victory over the sea-god Yam resulted in his attaining the kingship of the gods and whose 'seven lightnings..., eight storehouses of thunder' (probably a poetic way of saying 'seven lightnings and storehouses of thunder') are also attested in the Ugaritic texts. So great are the similarities between Psalm 29 and Canaanite Baal mythology that it has often been supposed that the psalm has simply appropriated a Canaanite Baal hymn and substituted the name Yahweh for Baal. However, this is probably going too far, since v.11 sounds more Yahwistic than Baalistic ('May the Lord give strength to his people! May the Lord bless his people with peace!') so that even proponents of the above hypothesis sometimes regard this verse as a later addition, while v. 8 ('the Lord shakes the 'wilderness of Kadesh') sounds like an allusion to Yahweh's theophany at Sinai (cf. Exod. 19.16-18; Hab. 3.3-7). It is therefore preferable to regard Psalm 29 as modelled on Baal prototypes rather than simply reproducing a Baal psalm verbatim, with the mere substitution of Yahweh for Baal.

Psalm 19 functions as both a hymn and a wisdom (Torah) psalm, and ancient near eastern parallels will be pointed out below, in Chapter 4. As will be seen, an ancient near eastern sun-god hymn must underlie it, and in fact, such an origin shows how the two halves of the psalm hang together, since the sun was regarded as the source of law and justice (vv. 7ff.) as well as of light (vv. 4c-6).

Not only creation but also Yahweh's acts in history can be singled out to form the dominant theme of a hymn. This is the case in Psalm 105. However, though this is formally a hymn, the nature of its contents makes it more appropriate to consider it alongside Psalms 78 and 106 in the section on historical psalms (see Chapter 4).

Quite a number of psalms refer to Mt Zion and the temple, but there are six hymns which centre on Zion: Psalms 46; 48; 76; 84; 87 and 122. Psalms 84 and 122 may be termed pilgrim hymns, while Psalm 87 is the 'ecumenical psalm'. Psalms 46; 48 and 76 are a group which have in common the theme of the inviolability of Zion: nations are depicted coming up to besiege Zion and are miraculously defeated by Yahweh. This seems to be a cultic theme, dependent on a pre-Israelite, Canaanite tradition.

Another sub-category of the hymn consists of the enthronement psalms (Psalms 47; 93; 96–99), which celebrate Yahweh's enthronement as king. These are discussed in considerable detail below in Chapter 5.

Individual Thanksgiving Psalms

Their relation to Hymns and Individual Laments

One of the major types of psalm analysed by Gunkel was that
of individual thanksgiving, and he also identified a smaller
number of communal thanksgiving psalms. Thanksgiving
psalms thank and praise God for a specific act of deliverance
that the psalmist has experienced, whereas the hymns praise
God more generally for his attributes and deeds. This terminology has generally been followed up to the present day. C.
Westermann, however, has argued that there is no separate
genre of thanksgiving psalms completely distinct from what
have been called hymns. According to Westermann both are
psalms of praise, and what had hitherto been referred to as
hymns he calls descriptive psalms of praise, and what had
hitherto been referred to as thanksgiving psalms he calls
declarative psalms of praise. He claims that Hebrew lacks a
distinctive word for 'thank'; the verb *hôdâ* which has often
been translated 'to thank', rather means 'to praise'.

There certainly are points of contact between what have
traditionally been called hymns and what have been called
thanksgiving psalms, and a number of scholars have adopted
Westermann's new terminology for them. Most, however,
appear content to use the old terminology, which does have the
advantage of being clearer and more straightforward. The
most detailed criticism of Westermann has come from
another German scholar, F. Crüsemann. He insists that we
should continue to maintain the identity of a class of individual
thanksgiving psalms completely separate from the hymns,
since the former (in origin, at least) were recited in connection
with the *tôdâ* (thank-offering) sacrifice, thus giving them a
distinct *Sitz in Leben.* He further argues that contextual
evidence supports a meaning for *hôdâ* closer to 'thank' than to
'praise', since it denotes a response to a particular deliverance.
(On the other hand, Crüsemann fails to find any communal
thanksgiving psalms in the Psalter. See below.)

Unlike the hymns, the individual thanksgiving psalms
stand in a special relationship with the individual laments, the
two constituting as it were the two shells of a mussel. The
psalmists in the individual laments promise God that they will

sing a psalm of thanksgiving (cf. Pss. 7.17; 13.5; 26.12; 35.28), and perform their vows by a thank-offering or the like (cf. Pss. 27.6; 54.6-7; 56.12; 61.8), should their pleas result in a successful deliverance from distress. (For the thank-offering, see Lev. 7.11ff.; 22.29f.) The individual thanksgiving psalms represent the response to Yahweh's answering the prayers of lament, and sometimes also refer to the thank-offering (Ps. 107.22; 116.17; Jon. 2.9) or other sacrifices such as vows (cf. Pss. 66.13-15; 116.14, 18; Jon. 2.9). Ps. 116.13 also refers to the cup of salvation, which is usually thought to indicate a drink offering rather than being a mere metaphor. (This interpretation is supported by the depiction of the Phoenician king Yehawmilk of Byblos' lifting up a libation cup before the goddess Ba'alat, accompanying his description of her answering his prayer. See *ANEP*, pl. 477 and *ANET*, 656.)

The psalms which are commonly allotted to the individual thanksgiving genre are as follows: Psalms 30; 32; 34; 41; 116; 138; plus what are now simply parts of Psalms 40 (vv. 1-10) and 66 (vv. 13-20). Psalms 18 and 118 are also individual thanksgiving psalms in form, though the former is certainly a royal psalm so far as content is concerned, and the latter is also sometimes so regarded. However, although the subject of Psalm 118 appears to have some representative function, there are problems in equating him with the king, since the psalm seems to be a post-exilic composition, at any rate in its present form: 'the house of Aaron' mentioned in v. 3 most naturally refers to the post-exilic priests, who at that period were regarded as the 'sons of Aaron', in contrast to the pre-exilic period, when they were equated with the tribe of Levi as a whole. Psalm 107 is a general thanksgiving psalm for various groups of individuals, though in its final form (cf. vv. 2-3) it seems to have been adapted for the returning exiles (see below).

It will be noted that there are far fewer individual thanksgiving psalms than individual laments. Gunkel plausibly contended that this is to be put down to human nature, and in fact requests are more common than thanksgivings in prayer generally. It should be noted that individual thanksgiving psalms are even rarer proportionately in Babylonia, though a large number of Babylonian hymns are attested. The Old

Testament Psalter also contains a large number of hymns, and this may partly account for the relatively small number of individual thanksgiving psalms.

Basic Structure

It is frequently stated in the textbooks that the individual thanksgiving psalms typically have the following structure: (i) an introduction, in which the psalmist states his intention to thank Yahweh, (ii) a narrative, in which the psalmist describes (a) his previous lamentable condition, (b) his prayer to Yahweh for deliverance, (c) Yahweh's act of deliverance, and (iii) a conclusion. This full form is rather well represented by Psalm 116.

(i)	v. 1	'I love the Lord . . . ' (instead of the usual reference to thanks or praise)
(iia)	v. 3	'The snares of death encompassed me, The pangs of Sheol laid hold on me; I suffered distress and anguish.'
(iib)	v. 4	'Then I called on the name of the Lord: 'O Lord, I beseech thee, save my life!'
(iic)	v. 6b	'when I was brought low, he saved me'.
(iii)	vv.12-19	Hymnic conclusion in which the psalmist promises to pay vows and offer a sacrifice of thanksgiving.

However, it should be noted that there is in fact a large amount of variation within the structures of the individual thanksgivings. Sometimes the 'introduction' is completely missing or is replaced by sentiments starting 'Blessed is he . . . ' Sometimes not all three of the elements in the 'narrative' are explicitly present, and the order in which they occur can differ. Finally, there is considerable variety in the concluding section.

Individual thanksgiving psalms could be recited in a variety of situations. One important context was that of recovery from illness, and this is also attested outside the Psalter in the prayer of Hezekiah in Isa. 38.10-20 and in Job 33.19-28. Within the Psalter the most vivid and explicit example is Psalm 41. A large part of this psalm is taken up with recounting the

original lament and the surrounding circumstances (vv. 4-
10), to such an extent that some scholars prefer to interpret
the psalm as a whole as a lament. However, most think that
vv. 11-12 (cf. vv. 1-3) presuppose that the psalmist has
recovered. (Verse 13 is the doxology concluding the first book of
the Psalter.) Other psalms of thanksgiving for recovery from
illness are to be found in Psalms 30 and 32 (cf. Ps. 107.17-22).
Note the references to Sheol and the Pit (i.e. the underworld)
in Psalm 30, such as are also found in some individual laments
concerned with illness (vv. 2-3, 8-9). (Interestingly, the
Egyptian thanksgiving psalm of Nebre, which thanks the god
Amon for the deliverance of his son from illness, similarly
speaks of this as a rescue from the underworld [*ANET*, 380].)
Psalm 116 has also sometimes been seen as a thanksgiving for
recovery from illness, as might be suggested by the Sheol
imagery of v. 3 and by v. 8, 'For thou hast delivered my soul
from death... ' However, K. Seybold thinks that the statement
that 'Men are all a vain hope' (v. 11b) and the confession
'Thou hast loosed my bonds' (v. 16) suggest otherwise.

The precise settings for the other individual thanksgiving
psalms are also not entirely clear, though Psalms 18 and 118
(the former certainly a royal psalm) clearly relate to some
conflict with foreign nations and will be discussed elsewhere. It
is fairly clear, however, that individual thanksgiving psalms
could be recited in all manner of situations of deliverance from
distress. This fact is well illustrated by Psalm 107, which
depicts four such kinds of distress. To a consideration of this
psalm we must now turn.

Psalm 107: a unique Thanksgiving Psalm

Psalm 107 is a thanksgiving psalm that stands in a class of its
own. The central part (vv. 4-32) consists of four sections, each
telling of a group of individuals who were in distress: the first,
desert travellers smitten with hunger and thirst (vv. 4-9), the
second, prisoners (vv. 10-16), the third, those who were sick
(vv. 17-22), and the fourth, seafarers in a storm (vv. 23-32). Of
each of these groups in turn we read, 'Then they cried to the
Lord in their trouble, and he delivered them out of their distress' (vv. 6, 13, 19, 28), and each in turn is exhorted, 'Let them

thank the Lord for his steadfast love, for his wonderful works to the sons of men!' (vv. 8, 15, 21, 31). The final part of the psalm is a hymn, extolling the providence of God, who is lord over nature and human beings.

There is no universal agreement about the setting and development of this psalm, though most agree that it is not an original unity. The original psalm probably consisted of vv. 1, 4-32. This seems to presuppose a service at which various groups who have experienced Yahweh's salvation are exhorted to thank him. (There is no need to regard the section on the seafarer in vv. 23-32 as a later addition, as W. Beyerlin does—it is noteworthy that all four groups, including the seafarer, are mentioned together in the Babylonian Shamash hymn [*ANET*, 387-89]). Most probably vv. 2-3 are a later addition: 'Let the redeemed of the Lord say so, whom he has redeemed from the hand of the enemy and gathered in from the lands, from the east and from the west, from the north and from the south'. These verses are certainly an allusion to those returning from the exile and the diaspora (cf. Isa. 11.12; 43.5; 49.12), which does not fit well the four examples of distress cited if these are intended literally. Furthermore, it is clear from comparable examples in the Old Testament (Neh. 9.27; Job 6.23; Ps. 78.61; Lam. 1.7; Ezek. 39.23) that *miyyad ṣār* in Ps. 107.2 means 'from the hand of the enemy', not 'from the hand of distress', whereas elsewhere in Psalm 107 *ṣar* is used in the sense of 'distress' (vv. 6, 13, 19, 28). This again supports the view that there is a separate stratum in vv. 2-3. Presumably, when vv. 2-3 were added, the various types of distress were reinterpreted metaphorically—cf. Isa. 42.7; 49.9 for the imagery of the exile as a prison, Ps. 147.2-3; 2 Chron. 33.16, and probably also Isa. 53.4, where the exile is spoken of as a sickness, and Isa. 54.11, where the exiles are said to be storm-tossed. The hymnic ending of Psalm 107 (vv. 33-42) may also be presumed to be a later addition.

Communal Thanksgiving Psalms

This is the most nebulous of the psalm categories. No scholar attributes many psalms to this class—e.g. Gunkel included Pss. 66.8-12; 67; 124; 129; Westermann Psalms 124 and 129;

and Weiser only Ps. 124. Crüsemann has denied the existence of a class of communal thanksgiving psalms altogether, and sees those that have been attributed to it as belonging to other classes. In principle there is no reason why such psalms should not exist: just as the large number of individual lament psalms is paralleled by a much smaller number of communal laments, so one might expect the relatively small number of individual thanksgiving psalms to be paralleled by communal thanksgivings. The problem is to decide whether there are any and, if so, which these are. Part of the problem consists in the existence of a category of hymns (psalms of praise), since the distinction in principle between these and communal thanksgiving psalms is a rather fine one: in both, the nation praises or thanks God for his deeds, and it may be that the ancient Israelites did not clearly distinguish them in their minds in the manner of modern form critics! However, if one applies the criterion that hymns should contain general praise of God (whether for his creative activity or acts in history) and communal thanksgiving psalms should thank God for a specific act of deliverance in the recent past, then Psalm 124 would seem to belong to the latter category.

The fact that the word 'thank' is not explicitly included in the psalm is not a weighty argument against seeing this as a thanksgiving psalm (*contra* Crüsemann), since a number of the individual thanksgiving psalms also lack the word and use other words instead, including the root 'bless' as in Psalm 124 (see Psalms 34; 41). Clearly the idea of a communal thanksgiving to God for some deliverance is present in Psalm 124.

It is true that Psalm 129 has some points of similarity to Psalm 124 (e.g. the words 'let Israel now say' in v. 1 of each psalm), but it contains no explicit thanksgiving to Yahweh, and the second half of the psalm is taken up with imprecations on enemies. Perhaps it is best regarded as a communal psalm of confidence, as some have proposed. As for Psalm 67, this is perhaps better understood as a prayer for blessing (communal lament?) rather than a communal thanksgiving, since the first and last verses appear to be jussive—'May God be gracious to us and bless us... May God bless us'—which is strange if the psalm is thanking God for blessings already received.

What could lend support to the communal thanksgiving idea
is v. 6, where the use of the perfect verb (*nāt^enâ*) would naturally suggest the rendering 'The earth *has yielded* its
increase', but the parallel line's jussive declaration 'May God,
our God, bless us' (cf. too the next verse) could indicate that we
have what is called a precative perfect and we could then
translate 'May the earth yield its increase'. This would then be
in keeping with the rest of the psalm. Finally, with regard to
Ps. 66.8, 12, while these verses do have the form of a
communal thanksgiving, they are only part of a psalm, vv. 1-7
of which have the character of a hymn, while vv. 13-20 are an
expression of individual thanksgiving.

Further Reading

On the Psalms of Praise:

> R. Albertz, *Weltschöpfung und Menschenschöpfung*, Stuttgart:
> Calwer, 1974.
> F. Crüsemann, *Studien zur Formgeschichte von Hymnus und
> Danklied in Israel* (WMANT, 32), Neukirchen: Neukirch-
> ener Verlag, 1969, 1-154, 285-306.
> C.G. Cummings, *The Assyrian and Hebrew Hymns of Praise*,
> New York: Columbia University Press, 1934.
> J. Day, *God's Conflict with the Dragon and the Sea: Echoes of a
> Canaanite Myth in the Old Testament*, Cambridge: Cam-
> bridge University Press, 1985, 28-35, 51-53 (on Ps. 104), 57-60
> (on Ps. 29), and 120-22, 125-38 (on the Zion Psalms).
> D.R. Hillers, 'A Study of Psalm 148', *CBQ* 40 (1978), 323-34.
> P.D. Miller, *Interpreting the Psalms*, 64-78.
> S. Mowinckel, *The Psalms in Israel's Worship*, 1, 81-105.
> L. Sabourin, *The Psalms: Their Origin and Meaning*, 1, 179-243.
> C. Westermann, *Praise and Lament in the Psalms*.

On the Individual Thanksgiving Psalms:

> W. Beyerlin, *Werden und Wesen des 107. Psalms* (BZAW, 153),
> Berlin/New York: W. de Gruyter, 1979.
> F. Crüsemann, *Studien zur Formgeschichte von Hymnus und
> Danklied in Israel*, 210-84.
> H.L. Ginsberg, 'Psalms and Inscriptions of Petition and
> Acknowledgment', in *Louis Ginzberg Jubilee Volume*
> (English section), New York: American Academy for Jew-
> ish Research, 1945, 159-71.
> S. Mowinckel, *The Psalms in Israel's Worship*, 2, 31-43

H. Graf Reventlow, *Gebet im Alten Testament*, Stuttgart: W.
   Kohlhammer, 1986, 208-20.
K. Seybold, *Das Gebet des Kranken im Alten Testament*.
L. Sabourin, *The Psalms: Their Origin and Meaning*, 2, 109-40.
C. Westermann, *Praise and Lament in the Psalms*, 103-16.

On the Communal Thanksgiving Psalms:

F. Crüsemann, *Studien zur Formgeschichte von Hymnus und
   Danklied in Israel*, 155-209.
S. Mowinckel, *The Psalms in Israel's Worship*, 2, 26-30.
L. Sabourin, *The Psalms: Their Origin and Meaning*, 2, 189-207.
C. Westermann, *Praise and Lament in the Psalms*, 81-90.

4

PSALMS OF CONFIDENCE,
WISDOM AND TORAH PSALMS,
HISTORICAL PSALMS,
ENTRANCE LITURGIES,
AND PILGRIMAGE PSALMS

Psalms of Confidence

IT IS GENERALLY ACCEPTED that there is a small group of psalms which are best categorized as psalms of confidence or trust in Yahweh. There is some dispute as to the precise parameters of this class but certain psalms recur in everyone's list. Probably we should include Psalms 11; 16; 23; 27.1-6; 62 and 131, to which should be added Psalm 129 as a communal psalm of confidence, as has just been noted (see discussion in Chapter 3 under 'Communal Thanksgiving Psalms').

Expressions of confidence are, of course, encountered in other types of psalm. For instance, they often form a feature of the individual laments, and Gunkel supposed that it was from there that the expression of confidence was taken up and achieved independent form, with the lament itself becoming completely eliminated. Others see a closer connection with the psalms of thanksgiving. However, whilst having points of contact with each of these, the psalms of confidence are distinct from both. The psalmist neither requests God to deliver him from enemies or other evils, nor thanks him for having done so, but rather expresses confidence that God does so. There is a tendency for these psalms to have statements about God in the third person rather than direct address to him in the second person, though this is not entirely lacking.

A point of contact with the individual laments is found especially in Psalm 16, which begins 'Preserve me O God, for in
thee I take confidence'. Psalm 4 is also sometimes classified as
a psalm of confidence, but is perhaps better seen as an individual lament (cf. v. 1) in which the note of trust is particularly
marked. Psalm 27 as a whole, in its present form, is clearly an
individual lament psalm, but vv. 1-6 were probably originally
separate, and have the character of a psalm of confidence. The
psalms of confidence in the purest form are Psalms 11; 23 and
62, referring as they do to God entirely in the third person.

Psalm 23

Psalm 23, the best known of all psalms, depicts God's lovingkindness under two images, those of the shepherd (vv. 1-4)
and the gracious host (vv. 5f.). It has sometimes been supposed
that the image of God as a shepherd persists throughout the
whole psalm, but this view involves the unjustified emendation
of *šulḥān* 'table' to *šelaḥ* 'weapon' (the shepherd's club) in v. 5,
and problems are also created in having to make a sheep drink
from a cup in this verse! Others (e.g. D.N. Freedman) argue
that the underlying theme that binds the psalm together is
imagery drawn from the Exodus, but there is nothing about
this psalm that obviously suggests the Exodus. There is no need
to look for some underlying binding link between the two
halves of the psalm other than the lovingkindness of Yahweh
towards the psalmist.

The speaker of the psalm has sometimes been seen as a king,
especially because of the reference to the anointing of the
psalmist's head with oil in v. 5. However, this is unjustified,
since the verb used here for 'anoint' (*dšn*) is quite different
from that used elsewhere in connection with the king (*mšḥ*).
Nor is there good reason to believe that v. 5 is describing a
thank-offering banquet following the psalmist's deliverance,
as is sometimes supposed. The emphasis in v. 5 is clearly on the
divine grace towards the psalmist rather than the psalmist's
gratitude towards God.

Modern scholarship has shed light on this much-loved
psalm in a number of ways. For example, the traditional
'valley of the shadow of death' through which the psalmist

walks is now better rendered 'very dark valley' (we might say a 'death-dark valley') and the reference to the shepherd's rod and staff is illuminated by the custom of modern Palestinian shepherds of having two staffs—one a club to ward off robbers and wild animals and the other a staff to guide the sheep (cf. too Ezek. 37.16f. and Zech. 11.7ff.).

Wisdom and Torah Psalms

Wisdom Psalms

Almost all scholars agree that there is a category of psalms which can usefully be designated 'wisdom psalms', that is to say, psalms which have a certain kinship with the wisdom literature of the Old Testament (primarily Proverbs, Job and Ecclesiastes), and which we may presume were either composed or influenced by the sages. The criteria employed in distinguishing such psalms are both the presence of ideas characteristic of the wisdom books (e.g. concern for divine rewards and punishments, whether by way of affirmation or of Job-like questioning of their present operation) and the occurrence of linguistic and stylistic features distinctive of the wisdom literature (e.g. the use of the root *ḥkm* 'wise' or the word *ba'ar* 'brutishness'). The classification is thus not strictly a form-critical one but rather one based on content. While there is general agreement that wisdom psalms exist, and there is a core that occurs in everyone's list (e.g. Psalms 1; 37; 49), no two scholars seem to agree about the precise number of psalms to be included in this category. For example, according to S. Mowinckel, the wisdom psalms are Psalms 1; 34; 37; 49; 78; 105; 106; 111; 112; 127; according to R.E. Murphy they are Psalms 1; 32; 34; 37; 49; 112; 128; while R.N. Whybray includes Psalms 1; 19B; 37; 49; 51; 73; 90; 92; 94; 104; 107; 111; 119; and L. Perdue Psalms 1; 19A; 19B; 32; 34; 37; 49; 73; 112; 119 and 127.

Clearly a fair number of psalms betray a greater or lesser number of features suggestive of wisdom influence. The problem of the classification of particular psalms as wisdom psalms is due to the difficulty of deciding how many wisdom characteristics a psalm must possess before it may legitimately be so described. R.E. Murphy has attempted to bring methodological rigour into the discussion by distinguishing between wisdom psalms *per se* and psalms which, though belonging strictly to other genres, nevertheless betray some wisdom influence. Whether or not one agrees exactly with Murphy's tally of wisdom psalms, the distinction which he makes is clearly methodologically sound in principle.

Wisdom literature divides naturally into the more 'orthodox' type, comparable to the book of Proverbs, and the more questioning approach found in the books of Job and Ecclesiastes. The former type is confident of the just working of God's appointment of earthly rewards and punishments for the righteous and wicked, while the latter reflects varying degrees of questioning of this schematization of reality. Psalms 1 and 112 may be seen as wisdom psalms reflecting the former position and Psalms 37 and 49 (and possibly 73) the latter, though the Psalter contains nothing as sceptical as Ecclesiastes.

That Psalm 1 is a wisdom psalm is suggested by its opening expression *'ašrê* 'blessed', its concern with rewards and retribution and contrast of the righteous (*ṣaddîqîm*) and wicked (*rᵉšā'îm*), and its implicitly admonitory character. This is further supported by the fact that its comparison of the righteous with a flourishing tree has a striking parallel in the *Instruction of Amenemope*, an Egyptian wisdom book, where the wicked man is also compared to a tree (*ANET*, 422). (There is an Egyptian background to quite a lot of the wisdom in Proverbs, especially Prov. 22.17–23.11, which is also dependent on Amenemope.)

Psalm 112 is in some ways similar to Psalm 1 in its comparison of the fate of the righteous and the wicked (though here only the final verse refers to the wicked). It is an acrostic (alphabetical) psalm—a feature also found in certain other wisdom psalms—and it clearly forms a pair with Psalm 111 (another acrostic), a hymn influenced by wisdom, cf. v. 10, 'The fear of the Lord is the beginning of wisdom; a good understanding have all those who practise it'.

Psalms 37 and 49 (and possibly 73) are examples of more questioning wisdom psalms. They are all pervaded by the thought of the problem posed by the prosperity of the wicked

and the suffering of the righteous. All of them attempt to deal
with the problem by claiming that the prosperity of the wicked
is only ephemeral and that sooner or later the righteous will be
vindicated. Interestingly, Psalms 49 and 73 seem to envisage a
blessed life after death as part of the vindication of the righteous: 'But God will ransom my soul from the power of Sheol,
for he will receive me' (Ps. 49.15); 'Thou dost guide me with
thy counsel, and afterward thou wilt receive me to glory' (Ps.
73.24).

Torah Psalms

A sub-category of the wisdom psalms is that of what are
sometimes called Torah (Law) psalms, viz. Psalms 119, 19B,
and 1, the last of which has already been touched on. Like the
term wisdom psalm, the expression Torah psalm is also a
statement of content rather than form, but it is a useful category under which to include these psalms.

The Torah psalm *par excellence* is Psalm 119. The longest
psalm in the Psalter by far, it is acrostic in form. Each of the
first eight verses begins with the first letter of the Hebrew
alphabet, each of the next eight with the second letter, and so
on throughout all 22 letters, making 176 verses in all. To many
this psalm appears monotonous, repeating in many different
ways as it does the psalmist's devotion to the Torah in verse
after verse. Ten different terms for the Torah are used
throughout the psalm: eight major terms are employed, commandment (*miṣwâ*), statute (*ḥōq*) and word (*dābār*) 22 times
each, judgment (*mišpāṭ*) and testimony (*'ēdûṭ*) 23 times each,
precept (*piqqûd*) 19 times, law or instruction (*tôrâ*) 25 times,
way (*'ōraḥ*) once and way (*derek*) twice. Every verse in the
psalm has one of these terms, except vv. 90 and 122, while vv.
15, 16, 43, 160, 168 and 172 have two terms each. It is probably
not a coincidence that there are eight major terms in view of
the division of the psalm into groups of eight verses, though as
will be apparent from the figures, the psalm does not adhere
rigorously to the employment of one of each of the eight major
terms in every section. It is also striking that the concrete
specifics of the law are never spelled out.

Psalm 119 has rightly been described as anthological. It shows dependence on a number of other Old Testament books, including Deuteronomy, Proverbs and Jeremiah. It clearly reflects post-exilic legal piety, and its combination of legal piety and wisdom has something in common with the book of Ecclesiasticus (Ben Sira) in the Apocrypha. The psalm is *sui generis*—it is centred on the Torah, but has wisdom traits, as well as some features of the individual lament and occasionally of the hymn of praise.

Psalm 19 falls into two clearly distinct parts. Verses 1-6 testify to the creation as a witness to Yahweh's glory, and the sun in particular is singled out. Verses 7-14 extol Yahweh's Torah, by which one should live. It is the second half of this psalm which justifies its description as a Torah psalm. Five of the six terms for the law in vv. 7-9 occur also in Psalm 119, the one exception being 'the fear of the Lord'. Although the two halves of the psalm have often in the past been supposed to have originally been separate psalms, there is now good evidence that they belong together as an original unity. The sun-god in the ancient near east could be thought of not only as the source of light but also as the upholder of justice in the world (there is Sumero-Akkadian, Hittite and Egyptian evidence for this), and it seems likely that the two halves of Psalm 19 belong together in the context of the sun-god. See for example the Babylonian Shamash hymn (*ANET*, 387-89), which combines the natural and judicial functions of the sun-god Shamash. Moreover, many of the details in both parts of the psalm are paralleled in ancient near eastern sun-god literature (not only such points as the sun as bridegroom and mighty man, but also the various epithets used in connection with the Torah).

It has been suggested by some scholars, e.g. Mowinckel, that the wisdom and Torah psalms were not sung in the temple worship like other psalms but had a school setting, which is held to be more appropriate for their didactic character. We do not have a great deal of data to go by, but in general there seem to be inadequate reasons for assigning to the wisdom psalms quite a different setting from the rest of the Psalter. If the two halves of Psalm 19 inherently belong together as the evidence just presented suggests, then we have here a natural combination of the hymnic and the didactic, suggesting that the latter could indeed function in a context of worship.

It is intriguing to speculate whether the placing of two of the Torah psalms as Psalms 19 and 119 respectively represents deliberate editorial positioning. It is attractive to suppose so but certainty is not possible.

Historical Psalms

As with certain other psalm categories, e.g. royal, wisdom and Torah psalms, that of historical psalms is one not strictly based on criteria of form but rather of content. However, it does seem more useful to study Psalms 78; 105 and 106 together in view of their similar historical content, than to attempt to allot them to perhaps three separate form-critical categories, especially since it is not entirely clear to what other categories Psalms 78 and 106 would in fact be assigned. Psalm 106 has variously been described as a communal lament, a hymn, or a wisdom psalm, when in fact it fits none of these genres exactly. Psalm 105 is more obviously a hymn. All three psalms are notable for the length at which they recite Israel's earlier history, especially with regard to the Exodus, and the fact that Psalms 105 and 106 were placed next to each other indicates that the redactors saw them as standing together.

Psalm 78 has a didactic opening, but for the most part recites with an anti-northern bias the history of the Israelites from the Exodus (with special reference to the plagues and wilderness wanderings) to their defeat by the Philistines and Yahweh's abandonment of the Shiloh sanctuary c. 1050 BC. The rejection of the northern tribe of Ephraim (v. 67), encapsulated in that latter event, is contrasted with Yahweh's election of Zion and David (vv. 68ff.). The apparent reference to the eternity of the Solomonic temple (v. 69) indicates a pre-586 BC date. Further, the lack of mention of the fall of the northern kingdom, which would have clinched the psalmist's argument that Yahweh had rejected the north, suggests a date prior to 722 BC. The absence of reference to the fall of the northern kingdom also rules out the suggestion that Ps. 78 is a deuteronomistic psalm, since for the deuteronomists this event signalled God's final judgment on the north (cf. 2 Kgs 17). The psalmist knows precisely the seven plagues of the Yahwist (J) source of the Pentateuch (vv. 41-51) and this source has traditionally and probably rightly been regarded as the earliest, dating from the early monarchical period. Although a few scholars date the Yahwist in the exile, the complete absence of doom and gloom from the work tells against this, and indeed, the fact that a multiplicity of sanctuaries are regarded as legitimate strongly argues for a date prior to Deuteronomy and Josiah's centralizing reform of 621 BC. Indeed, our pre-722 BC dating for Psalm 78 implies a date no later than this for the Yahwist.

In contrast, Psalm 105 shows knowledge of the Priestly (P) and Elohistic (E) sources of the Pentateuch in its account of the plagues (vv. 28-36). Since P probably dates from the sixth century BC and parts of the psalm are quoted in 1 Chron. 16.8-22, a book generally dated to the fourth century BC, we have evidence that Psalm 105 dates from the early post-exilic period. After a hymnic introduction, we have a long recollection of Yahweh's acts from the divine promise of the land of Canaan to the patriarchs Abraham, Isaac and Jacob, through the period of the sojourn in Egypt under Joseph, the Exodus under Moses, with the plagues spelled out in detail, the wilderness wanderings, and finally the settlement in Canaan. The psalm ends with a hymnic conclusion. The placing of this psalm immediately after Psalm 104 is probably deliberate, since each in its own way extols at great length the divine activity in a particular sphere, Psalm 104 in creation and Ps. 105 in history.

Psalm 106 similarly dates from the post-exilic period, since it shows knowledge of the exile (vv. 27, 47). It is considerably different in tone, however, since whereas Psalm 105 is pervaded by a sense of praise and gratitude for Yahweh's gracious acts in the history of Israel, Psalm 106 is dominated by the thought of Israel's disobedience to Yahweh in the face of his gracious deeds. It also concentrates on the period of the Exodus, but draws attention to such events as the rebellion of Dathan and Abiram, the making of the golden calf, and the apostasy to the god Baal of Peor. This disobedience continued in Canaan, with idolatry even involving human sacrifice, leading to repeated judgments and finally exile, from the continuing effects of which deliverance is still sought. Although it is not strictly a communal lament, recitation of the psalm would doubtless have induced lament.

Finally, it should be noted that some scholars include Psalms 135 and 136 among the historical psalms. It is to be observed, however, that these two related psalms, in spite of a certain amount of recitation of history, also contain material pertaining to Yahweh's work in creation, and are much more pervaded by a spirit of praise, thus justifying their designation as hymns.

Entrance Liturgies

Psalm 15 is the only psalm which in its entirety may be said to constitute an entrance liturgy. The same structure is to be found in Ps. 24.3-6 and, by way of prophetic imitation, in Isa. 33.14-16. This structure consists as follows:

(a) Question about who may be admitted to the temple, Pss. 15.1; 24.3; cf. Isa. 33.14.
(b) Answer, setting out the ethical requirements, Pss. 15.2-5b; 24.4-5; cf. Isa. 33.15.
(c) Word of blessing with regard to those who are qualified to enter the temple, Pss. 15.5c; 24.6; cf. Isa. 33.16.

We seem to have here the reflection of a liturgy taking place at the entrance to the temple, in which the worshippers enquire of the priest concerning the qualifications necessary for entry into the holy place, and the priest replies by setting forth the ethical requirements, together with a word of blessing concerning those so qualified.

Whereas Psalm 15 as a whole is an entrance liturgy, Ps. 24.3-6 forms part of a larger liturgical piece involving a procession into the temple with the Ark, the symbol of Yahweh the divine king (vv. 7-10), who has been victorious over the chaos waters at creation (vv. 1-2). As such, it has its setting at the celebration of Yahweh's enthronement as king at the feast of the Tabernacles, on which see below, Chapter 5. Whatever the date of Psalm 15, Psalm 24 is certainly pre-exilic, as is shown by its reference to the Ark.

It is noteworthy that the emphasis in these entrance liturgies falls on ethical rather than ritual qualifications. Clearly, the moral qualities enumerated must represent typical virtues rather than constituting the sum total of those required. In Psalm 15 the ethical requirements listed appear to be ten in number (vv. 2-5b), which calls to mind the Decalogue.

Similar requirements are attested elsewhere in the ancient near east with regard to those who seek entrance to the sacred temples, though there ritual qualifications are also sometimes included.

Pilgrimage Psalms

That pilgrims went up to the temple on Mt Zion singing and playing music is indicated by Isa. 30.29 and Ps. 42.4. Two psalms clearly having a pilgrimage setting are Psalms 84 and 122, though from another point of view these may also be classified as Zion psalms (see above, Chapter 3). Psalm 122 forms one of a series of psalms headed 'song of the steps (or ascents)'. To a consideration of these we must now turn.

The Songs of the Steps (or Ascents)

Psalms 120–134 are a group of psalms all having the Hebrew superscription *šîr hamma'ᵃlôt*, with the exception of Psalm 121 which has *šîr lamma'ᵃlôt*. This heading is most commonly rendered 'Song of ascents', following the meaning of the singular *hamma'ᵃlâ*, 'the ascent', in Ezra 7.9, and these psalms are then understood as pilgrim songs. In favour of this view it can be pointed out that Psalm 122 looks very much like a pilgrim psalm: 'I was glad when they said to me, "Let us go to the house of the Lord!"... Jerusalem, built as a city which is bound firmly together, to which the tribes go up, the tribes of the Lord' (vv. 1, 3-4a). The verb 'go up' here (v. 4) is from the same root as the noun *ma'ᵃlôt*. Psalm 132 also involves a procession with the Ark to Jerusalem. It is possible, therefore, that these psalms constituted a collection of psalms that were employed in pilgrimages and processions to Jerusalem.

However, it is questionable whether the psalm heading should be translated 'song of ascents'. The meaning 'ascent' for *maʿlâ* is attested only in Ezra 7.9; in the overwhelming number of cases in the Old Testament the word means 'step' or 'stair' (often in connection with the temple), and this is how the word is understood in the Greek Septuagint and Latin Vulgate translations of our psalm headings. It is thus possible that these are psalms to be sung on certain steps associated with the temple. There seems to be support for this in the Mishnah: 'fifteen steps (*maʿlôt*) led up within it (i.e. the Court of the Women) to the Court of the Israelites, corresponding to the 15 songs of the steps (*maʿlôt*) in the psalms, and upon them the Levites used to sing' (*Middoth* 2.5; similarly in more detail, *Sukkah* 5.4). Although these references do not state explicitly that the psalms were sung on the steps, this would seem to be the implication, and in any case they certainly indicate that their superscription was understood to mean 'song of the steps'. Some scholars, while accepting this translation, prefer to associate the psalms with other steps, such as the steps of the hall which led to the interior of the temple, which was where the Aaronic blessing was pronounced (*Tosefta Sotah* 7.7), or 'the steps of the city of David' (Neh. 3.15; 12.37), which were the steps leading up to the city of Jerusalem. Since the heading most naturally means 'the song of the steps' and since, on the other hand, there is some evidence connecting these psalms with pilgrimages and processions, the most attractive suggestion is to suppose that these psalms were sung by certain pilgrims and processions as they went up to Jerusalem, perhaps by the steps of the city of David. But we lack sufficient evidence to be dogmatic.

There are two views, on the other hand, which may certainly be rejected. The first is that the title refers to the step-like nature of the parallelism in the poetry of these psalms; this is unlikely, since it is not peculiar to these psalms. The second view to be rejected is that the heading refers to the ascent of exiles returning from Babylon; against this stands the fact that some of the psalms imply that the city is rebuilt and the temple is already in use (e.g. Ps. 122.3-4, 7).

The psalms in question, though reflecting a wide range of form-critical types, do seem to have a number of features in common indicating that they are a homogeneous group. Thus, they are all short (with the exception of Psalm 132), tend to have concluding formulas and contain repetitions, make frequent reference to Zion, Israel, blessing and Yah (a short form of Yahweh), and use the particles *kēn* 'so' and *hinnēh* 'behold', the relative *še-* 'which', and Aramaisms. The last two points are clear indicators of a post-exilic date, which most of them are (though Psalm 132, with its reference to the king and the Ark, is pre-exilic).

The common view that associates these psalms with pilgrimages connects them with the three major festivals. C.C. Keet, however, preferred to relate them to pilgrims who were offering their first-fruits at the temple in accordance with Exod. 22.29; 23.19; 34.26. The Mishnaic reference in *Sukkah* 5.4 connects them with the feast of Tabernacles, and Mowinckel follows this, though his understanding of *ma'alôt* as meaning 'festal processions' (lit. 'ascents') is open to question. K. Seybold, who also sees these psalms as pilgrimage psalms, believes that they were originally part of popular peasant piety and that they subsequently underwent a Zionistic, liturgical redaction. However, in spite of the value of Seybold's study, this interpretation seems rather speculative and subjective.

L.J. Liebreich has noted some striking parallels between the Aaronic Priestly Blessing in Num. 6.24-26 and these psalms. He sees the psalms (with the exception of Psalms 124, 126 and 131, which he thinks were added to bring the total number of psalms up to fifteen, the number of words in the Priestly benediction) as being a commentary on the Priestly Benediction, in particular four key words: *yebārekekā* '(may he) bless you', *weyišmerekā* 'and (may he) keep you', *wîhunnekā* 'and (may he) be gracious to you', and *šālôm* 'peace'. Parallels to these expressions are found in Pss. 120.6-7; 121.3-8; 122.6-8; 123.2-3; 125.5; 127.1; 128.4-6; 129.8; 130.2, 6; 132.15; 133.3; 134.3. As we read in *Tosefta Sotah* 7.7 that the Aaronic Priestly Benediction was pronounced on the steps of the hall which led to the interior of the temple, Liebreich thinks that this provides the explanation of the expression *ma'alôt* 'steps' in the heading to the psalms. It must certainly be admitted that the parallels with the Aaronic Priestly Benediction are striking and are rather pervasive throughout these psalms, and it is attractive to suppose that they do reflect a similar milieu. One may also note the reference to Aaron in Psalm 134. However,

Liebreich's suggestion that three psalms were added to make the total up to fifteen, the number of words in the Priestly Benediction, seems somewhat artificial, and it should be pointed out that there are no parallels in these psalms to the parts of the Priestly Benediction which read 'The Lord make his face to shine upon you... The Lord lift up his countenance upon you'.

These psalms are attractive, and B. Duhm went so far as to say that they are the finest in the Psalter. Various phrases within them have become well known, e.g. 'Unless the Lord builds the house, those who build labour in vain' (Ps. 127.1), and the words traditionally rendered 'for he gives to his beloved sleep' (Ps. 127.3), though as J.A. Emerton has argued, this is better rendered 'surely he gives honour to him who he loves' ('The meaning of *šēnā'* in Psalm cxxvii', *VT* 24 (1974), 15-31).

Further Reading

On the Psalms of Confidence in general:

> H. Gunkel and J. Begrich, *Einleitung in die Psalmen*, 254-56.
> L. Sabourin, *The Psalms: Their Origin and Meaning*, 2, 90-109.

On Ps. 23 in particular:

> D.N. Freedman, 'The Twenty-third Psalm', in L.L. Orlin (ed.), *Michigan Oriental Studies in Honor of George G. Cameron*, Ann Arbor: Department of Near Eastern Studies, University of Michigan, 1976.
> A.R. Johnson, 'Psalm 23 and the Household of Faith', in J.I. Durham and J.R. Porter (eds.), *Proclamation and Presence. Old Testament Essays in Honour of Gwynne Henton Davies*, London: SCM, 1970, 252-71.
> A.L. Merrill, 'Psalm xxiii and the Jerusalem Tradition', *VT* 15 (1965), 354-60.
> E. Power, 'The Shepherd's Two Rods in Modern Palestine and in Some Passages of the Old Testament', *Biblica* 9 (1928), 434-42.

On the Wisdom Psalms:

> A. Hurvitz, 'Wisdom Vocabulary in the Hebrew Psalter: A Contribution to the Study of "Wisdom Psalms"', *VT* 38 (1988), 41-51.

S. Mowinckel, 'Psalms and Wisdom', *SVT* 3 (1955), 205-24.

S. Mowinckel, *The Psalms in Israel's Worship*, 2, 104-25.

R.E. Murphy, 'A Consideration of the Classification "Wisdom Psalms"', *SVT* 9 (1962), 156-67.

L. Perdue, *Wisdom and Cult* (SBL Dissertation Series, 30), Missoula: Scholars, 1977, esp. 261-343.

R.N. Whybray, *The Intellectual Tradition in the Old Testament* (BZAW, 135), Berlin/New York: de Gruyter, 1974.

On the Torah Psalms:

A. Deissler, *Psalm 119 (118) und seine Theologie* (Münchener theologische Studien, 1. Historische Abteilung, Band 11), Munich: Karl Zink, 1955.

J.D. Levenson, 'The Sources of Torah: Psalm 119 and the Modes of Revelation in Second Temple Judaism', in P.D. Miller, P.D. Hanson, S.D. McBride (eds.), *Ancient Israelite Religion. Essays in Honor of Frank Moore Cross*, Philadelphia: Fortress, 1987, 559-74.

J.L. Mays, 'The Place of the Torah-Psalms in the Psalter', *JBL* 106 (1987), 3-12.

B. de Pinto, 'The Torah and the Psalms', *JBL* 86 (1967), 154-74.

N. Sarna, 'Psalm XIX and the Near Eastern Sun-God literature', in *Fourth World Congress of Jewish Studies. Papers*, 1, Jerusalem: World Union of Jewish Studies, 1967, 171-75.

On the Historical Psalms (as well as historical motifs in the Psalms more generally):

J. Day, 'Pre-Deuteronomistic Allusions to the Covenant in Hosea and Psalm lxxviii', *VT* 36 (1986), 1-12.

E. Haglund, *Historical Motifs in the Psalms* (Coniectanea Biblica, Old Testament Series, 23), Lund: C.W.K. Gleerup, 1984.

J. Kühlewein, *Geschichte in den Psalmen* (Calwer theologische Monographien, Reihe A 2), Stuttgart: Calwer, 1973.

L. Sabourin, *The Psalms: Their Origin and Meaning* 2, 295-307.

On the Entrance Liturgies:

W. Beyerlin, *Weisheitlich-kultische Heilsordnung. Studien zum 15. Psalm* (Biblisch-theologische Studien, 9), Neukirchen: Neukirchener Verlag, 1985.

L. Sabourin, *The Psalms: Their Origin and Meaning*, 2, 324-30.

J.T. Willis, 'Ethics in a Cultic Setting', in J.L. Crenshaw and J.T. Willis (eds.), *Essays in Old Testament Ethics (J. Philip Hyatt in Memoriam)*, New York: Ktav, 1974, 145-69.

On the Pilgrimage Psalms:

C.C. Keet, *A Study of the Psalms of Ascents*, London: Mitre, 1969.

L.J. Liebreich, 'The Songs of Ascents and the Priestly Blessing', *JBL* 74 (1955), 33-36.

K. Seybold, *Die Wallfahrtspsalmen* (Biblische-theologische Studien, 3), Neukirchen: Neukirchener Verlag, 1978.

5

THE AUTUMN FESTIVAL

The Autumn Festival as a Time for Celebrating Yahweh's kingship or Enthronement

The Festival and its Date

IN THIS CHAPTER we shall be concerned with the question of what may or may not have occurred at the celebration of the feast of Tabernacles or Autumn festival in the Jerusalem cult. This is a subject which has evoked much controversy; but it is clearly an important topic which must be broached if we are to obtain an intelligent understanding of the psalms in the worship of ancient Israel.

The feast of Tabernacles was one of the three major festivals of the Israelite year at which all male Israelites had to appear at the sanctuary, according to the pre-exilic sources (Exod. 23`.14-17; 34.22-23; Deut. 16.16). It was held in the autumn in September/October at the time of the ingathering of fruit, wine and oil, the other two festivals being held in the spring, namely the feast of Unleavened Bread (which came to be associated with Passover) at the time of the barley harvest in March/April, and the feast of Weeks (or Pentecost) at the time of the wheat harvest in May/June. In origin these were clearly all agricultural festivals which must have been appropriated from the Canaanites. The earliest cultic calendars which mention these feasts occur in Exodus 34, generally thought to be from the J or Yahwist source (traditionally dated to the tenth or ninth century BC) and in Exodus 23, commonly believed to emanate from the E or Elohistic source (traditionally dated to the eighth century BC). In Exod. 34.22

the feast of Tabernacles is said to take place at *t^eqûpat haššānâ* 'the coming round of the year', while in Exod. 23.16 it is stated to occur *b^eṣē't haššānâ* 'at the going out of the year'. Scholars have disputed whether these expressions refer to the beginning or the end of the year. Mowinckel claimed that Exod. 23.16 should be understood as referring to the time 'at the going forth of the year', i.e. the beginning of the year, in keeping with his thesis that the feast of Tabernacles had the nature of a New Year festival. However, the most careful survey of parallel expressions undertaken by E. Kutsch ('" ... am Ende des Jahres"', *ZAW* 83, 1971, 15-21) shows that when the root *yṣ'* is used of day, night, month or year in biblical Hebrew and Akkadian, it refers to its end, so that *b^eṣē't haššānâ* should be rendered 'at the going out (i.e. end) of the year'. This is consonant with the fact that in both Exodus 23 and 34. Tabernacles is mentioned last in the list of the three major festivals.

However, the fact that the expression *teqûpat haššānâ* 'the coming round of the year' is used of the feast of Tabernacles does suggest that this festival effectively marked the time when one year ended and another began. Possibly the last day of the festival marked the beginning of the new year. In other words, as well as marking the end of one year, it also appears to have heralded the beginning of the new year in pre-exilic Israel.

It should be noted that D.J.A. Clines has argued that the expressions in Exodus 23 and 34 merely refer to the turning point in the agricultural year rather than the calendar year. However, this is unlikely, since we know that later Judaism celebrated the New Year (and still does) in the autumn on 1st Tishri, even though technically the calendar year began in the spring. This is inexplicable on Clines' theory. In connection with what has just been said, it should be mentioned that in the post-exilic Old Testament literature we find Babylonian month names employed. These, it is generally recognized, were taken over by the Jews either in exile in Babylon in the sixth century BC or a few years before when the kingdom of Judah was under Babylonian hegemony. The Babylonian calendar presupposes a spring New Year, which explains why in the post-exilic Old Testament literature the feast of Tabernacles is said to take place in the 7th month (cf. Lev. 23.34). In contrast to this, in the pre-exilic period, the feast of Tabernacles took place at the time when one year ended and the new year began. This presupposes the autumnal calendar, corresponding to an important turning point in the agricultural year, and was clearly adopted from the Canaanites when the Israelites settled in the land.

What may or may not have happened at this festival is a much discussed subject. It was first argued by P. Volz in 1912, and independently by Mowinckel in 1922, that the Autumn Festival in Israel involved a celebration of Yahweh's primeval victory over the chaos waters at creation and his subsequent enthronement as king. This took place in the Jerusalem cult, Yahweh's presence being symbolized by the Ark, which was carried in procession up into the temple. In re-enacting Yahweh's primeval enthronement over chaos, the Israelites experienced it sacramentally anew, and looked to Yahweh to control the forces of chaos in the present so as to ensure both the fertility of the land and their political welfare. Psalms such as 47, 93 and 96–99 (the so-called enthronement psalms) were sung then, as well as many others, and it was argued that *Yahweh mālak,* which occurs in most of these psalms, should be rendered 'Yahweh has become king' rather than 'Yahweh is king', as had previously been supposed. The Babylonian New Year (Akitu) festival was appealed to as an analogy, for in this celebration the so-called Babylonian creation epic (*Enuma elish*) was recited, which recounts the god Marduk's victory over the watery chaos monster Tiamat and the creation of the world, with which his enthronement as king was associated. However, it is incorrect to suppose, as has sometimes been claimed, that Mowinckel simply read back the Babylonian festival into the Old Testament. On the contrary, he appealed primarily to various hints in the biblical text and also to later rabbinic evidence to support his reconstruction, and the Babylonian New Year festival was seen merely as a confirmatory analogy.

In the following sections we shall systematically survey the evidence that has been brought forward to support the notion that the feast of Tabernacles had the character of an enthronement festival in ancient Israel. In the course of this

we shall also examine the arguments which have been
brought against this thesis.

Post-exilic Evidence Supporting the Connection of the
Feast of Tabernacles/New Year with the
Celebration of Yahweh's Kingship

First, various pieces of post-exilic evidence can be cited indicating the connection of the theme of Yahweh's kingship with the
feast of Tabernacles or New Year.

(a) We know that in post-biblical Judaism Yahweh's kingship was (as indeed it still is) an important theme of the Jewish
New Year festival. Passages about Yahweh's kingship (the so-
called *Malkiyyoth*) are recited on this day, including Ps. 93.1
(one of the enthronement psalms) and the related Ps. 24.7-10.
Other verses recited are the *Shofaroth* (passages referring to
the blowing of the shofar or ram's horn), again including
verses from the two enthronement psalms, Pss. 47.5 and 98.6,
as well as the related Ps. 81.3. The earliest allusions to the
benedictions in connection with the Jewish New Year are in
the Mishnah, *Rosh hashshanah* 4.5. This is admittedly quite
late evidence, but as will be seen, further evidence supports its
antiquity.

(b) The heading to Psalm 29 in the Septuagint, the Greek
translation of the Old Testament, connects the psalm with the
feast of Tabernacles. Psalm 29 is a psalm pervaded by the
theme of Yahweh's kingship (cf. v. 10) and is clearly related to
the enthronement psalms in its motifs (cf. vv. 3, 10 with Ps.
93.3f., and vv. 1f. with Ps. 96.7-9).

(c) Zech. 14.16f. specifically connects the feast of Tabernacles
with the worship of Yahweh as king. We there read, 'Then
every one that survives of all the nations that have come
against Jerusalem shall go up year after year to worship the
King, the Lord of hosts, and to keep the feast of Tabernacles.
And if any of the families of the earth do not go up to
Jerusalem to worship the King, there will be no rain upon
them.' Although this passage is sometimes dismissed as late
(though it is in any case not as late as the evidence cited above),
it should be noted that (i) it may well not in fact be as late as
some supposed—P.D. Hanson, for example dates it between

475 and 425 BC; (ii) the cult tends to be very conservative, so that Zech. 14.16f. probably reflects much older ideas. The statement with regard to those who do not go up to the feast of Tabernacles that 'there will be no rain upon them' reflects the original agricultural nature of the festival, and encourages one to believe that other ancient aspects of it are also here adduced; (iii) as we shall see below, there is other earlier evidence which supports the connection between Yahweh's kingship and the feast of Tabernacles.

The Date of the Enthronement Psalms and their Relation to Deutero-Isaiah

An argument used by some scholars in opposition to Mowinckel's theories about these psalms is that they are post-exilic, being dependent on the prophet of the exile known as Deutero-Isaiah (Isaiah 40–55), whose message has some striking parallels with them (so, e.g., the early Kraus, N.H. Snaith, Westermann). They point out that Deutero-Isaiah's message, like that of the psalms in question, is pervaded by the thought of Yahweh as creator (e.g. Isa. 40.12, 28; cf. Pss. 93.1; 96.5, 10), and his superiority over other gods (e.g. Isa. 45.21f.; 46.9; cf. Pss. 96.4f.; 97.7, 9). The common refrain of the enthronement psalms (Pss. 47.8; 93.1; 96.10; 97.1; 99.1) is echoed in Isa. 52.7 *mālak* *ᵉlōhāyik*, 'your God has become king', and Yahweh's victory over the chaos waters is alluded to in both Ps. 93.3f. and Isa. 51.9f. There are even verbatim parallels: 'O sing to the Lord a new song' (Pss. 96.1; 98.1; Isa. 42.10), 'all the ends of the earth have seen (or shall see) the salvation of our God' (Ps. 98.3; Isa. 52.10), and 'let the sea roar and all that fills it' (Pss. 96.11; 98.7; Isa. 42.10 emended). Further parallels are found in the expressions 'his holy arm' (Ps. 98.1; Isa. 52.10), 'in the sight of the heathen' (Ps. 98.2; Isa. 52.10), 'clap their hands' (Ps. 98.8; Isa. 55.12), 'from of old' (Ps 93.2; Isa. 44.8; 45.21; 48.3, 5, 7f.), and the appeal to nature to join in the song of praise to Yahweh (Ps. 96.11f.; Isa. 44.23; 49.13).

These parallels certainly indicate some kind of connection between the psalms and Deutero-Isaiah, but do they prove that it was the prophet who was dependent on the Psalter? Could it not be, as other scholars claim, that it was Deutero-Isaiah who was dependent on the psalms? We have here a classic chicken and egg situation—which came first? A majority of scholars would today accept that at least some of the enthronement psalms are pre-exilic, and those who see dependence of the psalms on the prophet tend to limit this to Psalms 96 and 98, where the verbal parallels are closest (e.g. Jörg Jeremias). However, these too could well be pre-exilic, as we shall see.

A considerable number of arguments can be put forward in favour of the priority of the psalms in question. One weighty argument is the fact that Deutero-Isaiah was a absolute monotheist, who declares in no uncertain terms that there is no God in existence apart from Yahweh (cf. Isa. 44.6; 45.5, 14, 21; 46.9), whereas the psalms imply rather that the other gods exist but that Yahweh is superior to them (Pss. 96.4f.; 97.7, 9; cf. the related Ps. 95.3). If the psalms were dependent on Deutero-Isaiah, we should expect them to reflect his strong monotheism; as it is, they represent the kind of belief characteristic of the period prior to the exile. Some of Deutero-Isaiah's other distinctive themes are also lacking in these psalms, and this would be surprising if they were dependent on him. For example, the motifs of Yahweh as 'redeemer' (*gō'ēl*) and of the new Exodus are missing, and there are no references to Babylon, the captivity there or the restoration after the exile. The precise nature of the event causing the 'new song' is not spelled out. As for the words 'O sing to the Lord a new song' (Pss. 96.1; 98.1; Isa. 42.10), these are characteristic of psalmody rather than prophecy (cf. Pss. 33.3; 40.3; 144.9), thus suggesting the priority of Psalm 96 or 98 (whichever is the source) over Deutero-Isaiah. This important point appears not previously to have been noted. Add to this the fact that there is abundant evidence elsewhere of Deutero-Isaiah's dependence on psalmic forms and themes, and it becomes difficult to deny that it is the prophet who has taken up motifs from the enthronement psalms and applied them to the contemporary situation: Yahweh's kingship is to be manifested anew in the overthrow of Babylon and the deliverance of the Jewish exiles, vindicating the God of Israel over other gods and bringing about the inauguration of a new age.

In the course of the above discussion, it has emerged that Psalms 96; 97 and 98, as well as the related Psalm 95, are likely to be earlier than Deutero-Isaiah. The same is true of the other enthronement psalms. Thus, Psalm 47 is widely agreed to be pre-exilic, since 'God has gone up with a shout, the Lord with the sound of a horn' (v. 5) implies a ceremony with the Ark (see below), and there was no Ark in the post-exilic period. Again, something like Psalm 99 with its threefold reference to Yahweh's holiness (vv. 3, 5, 9), in the context of Yahweh's kingship and the quaking of the earth (v. 1), seems to lie behind Isaiah's call vision in the temple (Isa. 6.1-4). Furthermore, v. 1 speaks of Yahweh's being 'enthroned upon the cherubim'. If this alludes to the cherubim in the temple rather than the heavenly cherubim, as the reference to his being 'great in Zion' in the next verse suggests, then Yahweh's 'footstool' in v. 5 will be the Ark in the temple beneath the cherubim throne, so that a pre-exilic date will again be indicated. As for Psalm 93, this is widely believed to be an early psalm, as its depiction of Yahweh's victory over the chaotic waters stands close to the underlying Canaanite myth.

All in all, therefore, there are good reasons for believing that the enthronement psalms are anterior to Deutero-Isaiah and reflect the worship of the Jerusalem cult in the pre-exilic period.

The Setting of the Enthronement Psalms in the Pre-exilic Period

Granted that the enthronement psalms are pre-exilic, is there evidence to support their setting in the feast of Tabernacles/New Year in that period in the way that we have already seen to be the case in the post-exilic era? Indeed there is.

(a) First, it is to be noted that the theme of Yahweh's kingship was closely associated with that of the creation of the world. This is true both of psalms containing the idea of Yahweh's kingship which are not specifically enthronement psalms (cf. Pss. 24.1f., 7ff.; 74.12ff.) as well as of the enthronement psalms themselves (Pss. 93.1f.; 96.10; cf. 95.3-6). Since the creation would naturally have been thought of as having taken place at the time of the very first new year, the time around the new year was clearly the most appropriate period in which to recall Yahweh's creative activity. As we have seen, it was at about this time that the feast of Tabernacles occurred, according to the pre-exilic sources (cf. Exod. 23.16; 34.22). Indeed, these psalms would have been far more appropriately associated with Tabernacles in the pre-exilic period than later, since in the post-exilic period, when the spring calendar was in force, the feast of Tabernacles fell in the seventh month (cf. Lev. 23.34), whereas in the pre-exilic era it took place at the time when one year ended and the next began. No better setting for the enthronement psalms and other psalms about Yahweh's kingship can therefore be envisaged. In keeping with this, the general sense of the newness of things that pervades these psalms should be borne in mind—cf. Pss. 96.1 and 98.1, 'O sing to the Lord a *new* song...'

(b) Secondly, it should be noted that there are a number of allusions to the Ark being carried in procession at the time when Yahweh's kingship was being celebrated (Pss. 24.7ff.; 47.5; 68.1 [cf. Num. 10.35], 18). This bringing up of the Ark was at least in part a recapitulation of David's bringing the Ark up into Zion in 2 Sam. 6, which is re-enacted in Psalm 132. (Interestingly, 1 Chron. 16.23-33 cites Psalm 96, one of the enthronement psalms, in its entirety as one of the psalms sung in connection with David's action.) Now, the Ark was finally brought up into the temple by Solomon, and it is surely significant that this is specifically dated to the time of the feast of Tabernacles in 1 Kgs 8.2 ('the feast in the month of Ethanim, which is the seventh month'). We thus have here another pointer to the connection between Yahweh's kingship and the feast of Tabernacles in the pre-exilic period.

Overall, therefore, we have produced three independent converging pieces of evidence supporting the view that Yahweh's kingship was associated with Tabernacles/New Year in the post-exilic period and a further two independent converging pieces of evidence indicating that Yahweh's kingship was likewise connected with Tabernacles/New Year in the pre-exilic era. Whilst each piece of evidence, taken alone, might not seem compelling, taken together these five arguments add up to a plausible case. A high degree of plausibility attaches to Mowinckel's theory that the celebration of the kingship of Yahweh was an important part of the ancient Israelite feast of Tabernacles/New Year. Moreover, those scholars who reject this view have failed to produce a more convincing setting for the enthronement psalms. Thus N.H. Snaith saw them as Sabbath psalms; but as Mowinckel pointed out, there is nothing at all in these psalms to suggest that the Sabbath was their original setting. They centre on Yahweh's activity rather than his rest! Again, S. Aalen thought that they were 'morning psalms', i.e. psalms composed for the daily morning sacrifice (the *tāmîd*) in the temple, but this theory too lacks evidence.

The Meaning of *Yahweh mālak* and *mālak ᵉlōhîm*: Yahweh/God is King or Yahweh/God has become King?

The psalms commonly called enthronement psalms are Psalms 47; 93; 96–99. In most of these we find the declaration *Yahweh mālak* (Pss. 93.1; 96.10; 97.1; 99.1) or, in the case of Ps. 47.8, *m ālak 'el ōhîm*. Mowinckel claimed that these expressions are to be translated respectively 'Yahweh has become king' and 'God has become king', and this understanding became important in support of his view of the Autumn Festival as a time at which Yahweh's enthronement was celebrated. Some scholars have rallied to Mowinckel's support, whereas others argue that *Yahweh mālak* should rather be rendered 'Yahweh is king' and some (though a smaller number) claim that *mālak ᵉlōhîm* means simply 'God is king'. Is there any way of deciding which of these views is correct? We shall now consider the arguments.

(a) Philologically it can be stated that the verb *mlk* is capable of meaning both 'to be king' and 'to become king'. If we exclude the controversial psalm passages under discussion as well as the related verse in Isa. 52.7, we may say that there are in fact three ways in which the perfect of the verb is employed:

(i) The perfect *mālak* is frequently used in the sense '(he) was king', as often in the books of Kings (e.g. 'Baasha the son of Ahijah... was king (*mālak*) twenty-four years', 1 Kgs 15.33).

(ii) The perfect *mālak* is also frequently used in the sense '(he) became king', again often in the books of Kings. For instance, 'In the third year of Asa king of Judah, Baasha the son of Ahijah became king (*mālak*) over all Israel in Tirzah...' (1 Kgs 15.33).

(iii) The perfect *mālak* is also found with the meaning '(he) has become king' in the context of royal coronations. For instance, 'and they blew the trumpet, and proclaimed, "Jehu has become king (*mālak*)"' (2 Kgs 9.13). Similarly 2 Sam. 15.10, and, subsequently to coronations, 1 Sam. 12.14; 1 Kgs 1.11, 13, 18.

Evidence of usage outside the psalms thus attests the meanings '(he) was king', '(he) became king' and '(he) has become king' for the perfect form *mālak*. Naturally no one suggests either of the first two meanings for the expressions *Yahweh mālak* or *mālak 'elōhîm* in the psalms, while Mowinckel's understanding is clearly rooted in the third. Form-critically, it is certainly the case that the coronation proclamations 'Jehu has become king' (*mālak yēhû'*) in 2 Kgs 9.13 and 'Absalom has become king' (*mālak 'absālôm*) in 2 Sam. 15.10 provide the closest parallels to *mālak 'elōhîm* and *Yahweh mālak*. If so, we have justification for Mowinckel's claim that the psalms under discussion are rightly termed enthronement psalms.

In spite of the evidence produced above, probably a majority of scholars opt for the rendering 'Yahweh is king' over against Mowinckel. Often no reasons are given for this rendering apart from the general feeling that it is more natural than 'Yahweh has become king'. However, whilst it may be more natural from the point of view of modern religious presuppositions, it is not the most natural from the point of view of the linguistic usage of *mālak* elsewhere in the Old Testament. Although it is well attested in Hebrew that verbs in the perfect can have a present meaning, so that '(he) is king' is in principle quite possible for *mālak*, this meaning is nowhere clearly found in the Old Testament. Rather, when the meaning of *mlk* is 'to be king', the perfect has to be rendered '(he) was king', as the examples cited above illustrate. Of course, it is perfectly possible to render the coronation proclamations in 2 Kgs 9.13 and 2 Sam. 15.10 as 'Jehu is king' and 'Absalom is king', but the enthronement contexts make it clear that what this would mean is 'Jehu is (now) king' and 'Absalom is (now) king'. The same is true of the declarations made about Adonijah in 1 Kings 1 immediately after his coronation, 'Adonijah has become king' (vv. 11, 13, *mālak ᵃdōnîyāhû*, v. 18 *ᵃdōnîyâ*

mālāk), and presumably also of the reference to Saul in 1 Sam.
12.14, 'the king who has become king over you' (*hammelek*
ᵃšer mālak ᵃlêkem), since this too comes in the context of the
chapters concerned with his enthronement (1 Sam. 8–12).
What we lack is a clear example where *mālak* simply means
'(he) is king' in a general, constant way without reference to a
recent enthronement.

The claim has, however, been made by J. Ridderbos and H.-J.
Kraus that the word order is significant in determining the
meaning of *mālak*. They maintain that when the verb is
placed first, the meaning is ingressive, so that *mālak ᵉlōhîm* in
Ps. 47.8 means 'God has become king' (cf. too *mālak ᵉlōhāyik*
'your God has become king' in Isa. 52.7), but when the subject
is placed first the meaning is durative, so that *Yahweh mālak*
(Pss. 93.1; 96.10; 97.1; 99.1) means 'Yahweh is king'.
Unfortunately there is no supporting evidence for this. As J.
Ulrichsen aptly points out, we find in the historical books of the
Old Testament expressions involving *mālak* in the sense '(he)
has become king' both with the subject first and with the verb
first: e.g. 1 Kgs 16.29 and 2 Kgs 15.13 follow the former order
and 1 Kgs 15.1 and 9 the latter. Rather, irrespective of the
precise meaning of the verb, L. Köhler is surely right that the
normal Hebrew word order is verb + subject, so that placing
the subject first gives it a certain emphasis. The emphasis
'*Yahweh* has become king' would certainly fit the content of
the enthronement psalms, stressing as they do Yahweh's
exaltation over the gods (Pss. 96.4f.; 97.7, 9; cf. 95.3), the chaos
waters (Ps. 93.3f.) and the nations (Pss. 98.2; 99.2).

(b) It is Psalm 47 which offers the clearest support for the
rendering 'has become king', so that some scholars accept it
for this psalm who would not for others. Three verses before
the words *mālak ᵉlōhîm* (v. 8) we read 'God has gone up with
a shout, the Lord with the sound of a horn' (v. 5). It is widely
accepted that this verse alludes to the carrying up of the Ark,
the symbol of Yahweh's presence, into the temple. Certainly no
other appropriate symbol of Yahweh's presence is known, and
the Ark appears to be attested elsewhere in connection with a
ceremony celebrating Yahweh's kingship in Pss. 24.7-10 and
68.1 (cf. words addressed to the Ark in Num. 10.35) and 68.18,
as well as in Psalm 132. Now the ceremony in Psalm 132

recapitulates the action of David in bringing the Ark up into Jerusalem in 2 Samuel 6, where we read that 'David and all the house of Israel brought up the Ark of the Lord with shouting, and with the sound of the horn', language recalling that of Ps. 47.5. This further confirms the Ark identification there. Since the Ark symbolizing Yahweh's presence would have been taken up into the temple and placed under the cherubim throne (cf. Ps. 99.1), it is natural to suppose that Ps. 47.8b should be rendered 'God has sat down on his holy throne' rather than 'God sits on his holy throne' and that the parallel line in v. 8a should similarly be translated 'God has become king over the nations' rather than 'God is king over the nations'. The whole context seems to imply an action rather than an eternal state.

That it is specifically an act of enthronement that Psalm 47 has in view is further supported by the reference to Yahweh's ascension in v. 5 being accompanied by the sound of a horn (*qôl šôpār*), for the sounding of a horn was a characteristic feature of Israelite coronation services as we know from 2 Sam. 15.10; 1 Kgs 1.34, 39, 41; 2 Kgs 9.13 (cf. too trumpets in 2 Kgs 11.14). Accordingly, it is natural to suppose, as Mowinckel has argued, that the words *mālak 'elōhîm*, to be translated 'God has become king', are modelled on the proclamations found in connection with the coronations of Israelite kings such as in the case of Jehu: *mālak yēhû'*, 'Jehu has become king' (2 Kgs 9.13).

Psalm 47 forms a particular embarrassment to Kraus. As an alternative to Mowinckel's enthronement festival, he sought to understand the Autumn Festival as a 'Royal Zion Festival', in which Psalm 132 was regarded as echoing the two central motifs of 2 Samuel 6–7, namely a procession with the Ark to the sanctuary and God's covenant promise to David. Although Kraus saw the entry of the Ark into the temple as being associated with the psalms about Yahweh's kingship, he denied that this had the character of an enthronement. He is clearly at a loss what to do with Psalm 47, since he admits that in this one psalm we do actually read of Yahweh's enthronement and he even finds it natural to suppose that the Ark is here referred to!

(c) In support of the view that 'Yahweh has become king' is the correct translation we may now further note the fact that the enthronement psalms are pervaded by a sense of the newness of things. This is explicitly the case in Psalms 96 and 98, the opening words of both of which are 'O sing to the Lord a *new* song'. That references to 'a new song' in psalmic passages characteristically indicate a new situation is demonstrated by the contexts in Pss. 40.3; 144.9; 149.1; and Isa. 42.10. In fact, the Isaianic allusion is an actual citation from Pss. 96.1, 11 and 98.1,7, and the preceding verse (Isa. 42.9), which speaks of God doing 'new things', makes the context clear. Accordingly, it is difficult to suppose that the expression *Yahweh mālak*, mentioned in connection with the 'new song' in these psalms, simply describes an eternal state ('Yahweh is king'), for there would be nothing new in that! As in Isa. 42.9f., a new era is surely in view, which makes the translation 'Yahweh has become king' the more likely rendering. The new era of God's rule is clearly described in Pss. 96.13 and 98.9: '... for he comes to judge the earth. He will judge the world with righteousness, and the peoples with equity (or his truth)'.

(d) Further evidence for the rendering 'Yahweh has become king' may be deduced from a consideration of the prehistory of the mythical concept underlying the enthronement psalms, which is especially visible in Ps. 93.3-4 (similarly Pss. 29.10; cf. v. 3) and 74.12-15. It is now clear that the Old Testament has here taken over and applied to Yahweh the Canaanite myth, known from the Ugaritic texts, of Baal's victory over the sea (Yam), as a result of which Baal became king (Gibson, 37-45). This tends to support the rendering 'Yahweh has become king' in v. 1. The related Babylonian myth of the god Marduk's defeat of the chaotic waters, recited at the Babylonian New Year festival, similarly relates how Marduk became king; but this event was a prelude to his victory rather than a consequence of it (*Enuma elish* 4.28 in *ANET*, 66).

(e) An additional supporting argument may be drawn from an examination of the post-psalmic understanding of Yahweh's kingship. Zechariah 14, which, as we have seen earlier, associates the celebration of Yahweh's kingship with the feast of Tabernacles (vv. 16f.), clearly envisages the eschatological coming of this kingdom in language echoing the enthronement psalms: 'And the Lord will become king over all the earth' (v. 9). This is clearly no static kingship but a dynamic one manifesting itself anew at the last time. Other themes of Zechariah 14 represent a projection forward of motifs from the psalms, e.g. the conflict with the nations (Zech. 14.1ff.; cf. Psalms 46; 48; 76), the mythical river of Jerusalem (Zech. 14.8; cf. Ps. 46.4), and the gathering of the nations to Jerusalem at the celebration of Yahweh's kingship (Zech. 14.16f.; cf. Ps. 47.9). The fact that Zech. 14.9 envisages Yahweh's *becoming* king over the earth in the future thus supports the ingressive understanding of *Yahweh mālak* in the enthronement psalms. Similarly in the New Testament Apocalypse, the declaration is made to God, 'Thou hast taken thy great power and begun to reign (*ebasileusas*)' (Rev. 11.17; cf. v. 15) and the cry goes up 'Hallelujah! For the Lord our God the Almighty has become king (*ebasileusen*)' (Rev. 19.6). It is interesting that *ebasileusen* corresponds precisely to the Septuagint's rendering of *mālak* in the enthronement psalms. One may also compare the words encapsulating the central message of Jesus, 'the Kingdom of God is at hand' (Mk 1.15), which similarly imply God's becoming king in the future in a sense not incompatible with his already in some way being king.

We have produced a number of arguments which cumulatively make a good case in support of Mowinckel's thesis that Psalms 47; 93; 96–99 celebrate not merely Yahweh's kingship but specifically his enthronement. The question has inevitably been raised by some scholars how one could speak of Yahweh's becoming king. After all, when was Yahweh not king? And who was capable of enthroning Yahweh? To the former question it may be replied that, if what is being proposed is that Yahweh was off the throne for part of the time, like the cyclically dying and rising gods of some near eastern fertility religions (e.g. Baal), then of course this would certainly be incompatible with Old Testament faith. While a few scholars have put forward such notions in the past (e.g. H. Schmidt, G. Widengren, S.H. Hooke), these views are now universally rejected. What Mowinckel and those who follow him have in mind is something quite different. It is accepted that Yahweh was regarded as king from primeval times; what the enthronement psalms are held to celebrate is the cultic re-enactment of Yahweh's primeval victory over chaos. Comparison has frequently been made with the annual repetition at Easter and Christmas services in the Christian Church of such phrases as 'Jesus Christ is risen today' and 'This day is born a Saviour, Christ the Lord'. However, the renewal of Yahweh's primeval kingship was held by Mowinckel to signify more than this: it betokened a reassertion of Yahweh's sovereignty over the powers of chaos now operative in history and nature, and also the goal towards which history was moving. A better Christian analogy for what Mowinckel had in mind may therefore be provided by the Eucharist, since this not only involves the re-enactment of a past event, but combines it with present experience as well as having future eschatological overtones.

An alternative to Mowinckel's understanding would be to see these psalms as simply eschatological, depicting Yahweh's future rule over the world, as Gunkel, Westermann, and Loretz have done. What are we to say of this? There are certainly eschatological overtones in the psalms, cf. Pss. 96.13 and 98.9, 'he will judge the world with righteousness and the peoples with truth (or equity)'. However, there are two objections to the view that the enthronement psalms are simply eschatological. First, the constant use of the phrase *Yahweh mālak* 'Yahweh has become king' would have to be taken as a 'prophetic perfect' (signifying a future event) throughout. It is strange that the psalmists could never have brought themselves to say outright 'Yahweh will become king' if that is what they meant. Secondly, the references to Yahweh's becoming king are closely associated with allusions to his creation of the world, as in Pss. 93.1 and 96.10, 'Yea, the world is established, it shall never be moved' (similarly, Ps. 95.4-5).

Mowinckel's view, which is not always properly understood, is, as has already been mentioned, that it is Yahweh's primeval victory at creation which is being celebrated, but in such a way that it is re-enacted and renewed in the present. One can appeal to a number of passages in support of this understanding. For example, Ps. 93.3 reads, 'The floods *lifted* up, O Lord, the floods lifted up their voice, the floods *lift* up their roaring'. The lifting up in the past seems to allude to the time of creation (spoken of in vv. 1 and 2), though the final line uses the present tense, 'the floods *lift* up their roaring'. Again, Ps. 65, which is clearly a harvest psalm associated with Tabernacles (it is still sung at harvest festivals today), moves from the thought of Yahweh's victory over the chaos waters at creation to the idea of his victory over the powers of chaos embodied in the enemy nations in the present: 'who by thy strength hast established the mountains, being girded with might; who dost still the roaring of the seas, the roaring of their waves, the tumult of the peoples' (vv. 6-7).

Finally, the question who would be in a position to enthrone Yahweh, may be answered by replying that this question is fundamentally misconceived, since in ordinary earthly coronations it is always the lesser who enthrones the greater, so no particular problem arises in the case of Yahweh's enthronement. It may be that the gods were thought of as enthroning Yahweh, or Yahweh may even have enthroned himself.

A Ceremony of Covenant Renewal?

The suggestion has been put forward by A. Weiser in his commentary on the Psalms—building on a proposal by G. von Rad—that the dominant theme of the Autumn Festival was not Yahweh's enthronement but rather covenant renewal, that is to say, the renewal of the covenant made between Yahweh and the Hebrew tribes under Moses on Mt Sinai. Weiser does not deny that Yahweh's enthronement was an element in the feast of the Tabernacles, but maintains that this was subordinate to the overall theme of covenant renewal. (Similarly, Mowinckel did not deny that covenant renewal was part of the enthronement festival, as he reconstructed it; indeed, it was he in 1927 who first argued this and suggested that the Decalogue had its origin in this festival.) It should be noted that Weiser included in his postulated festival a large number of psalms, in many of which it is far from obvious that the covenant idea is present.

What evidence is there for supposing that covenant renewal had any association with the feast of Tabernacles in ancient Israel? Two psalms which seem to presuppose covenant renewal on the basis of their contents are Psalms 50 and 81, and Jewish tradition expressly attests the connection of the latter with the autumnal New Year festival. The Jewish tradition is, of course, rather late evidence. Since, however, the late Priestly source of the Pentateuch associated the events of Mt Sinai rather with the feast of Weeks, and similarly the Qumran community later still connected covenant renewal with this festival, the divergent rabbinic tradition associating covenant renewal with Tabernacles may well hark back to an earlier state of affairs. That this is the case is supported by Deut. 31.9ff. Here we read, 'At the end of every seven years, at the set time of the year of release, at the feast of Tabernacles, when all Israel comes to appear before the Lord your God at the place which he will chose, you shall read this law before all Israel in their hearing'. Since Deuteronomy is the covenant book *par excellence*, we have here evidence going back at least to the sixth century BC associating covenant renewal with Tabernacles. Similarly, according to Neh. 8.2, Ezra read the book of the Law at the time of the autumnal New Year. Furthermore, it should be noted that both Ps. 81.7 (a covenant renewal psalm) and Ps. 95.8 (an enthronement psalm) make allusion to the sin in the wilderness at Massah and Meribah. We have already seen how much evidence connects the enthronement psalms with Tabernacles; the parallel allusion in Ps. 81 therefore serves to support the tradition of a comparable setting. A further, more general point that may be made is that, if one is going to renew the covenant, the time of the New Year (or New Year's Eve) is perhaps the best time to do so. Our custom of making New Year resolutions may be compared. The words of Ps. 81.3 certainly indicate the setting of the psalm at one of the three major festivals: 'Blow the trumpet at the new moon, at the full moon, on our feast day'. Such evidence as we have suggests that this was Tabernacles/New Year.

Psalm 81.9-10 echoes the beginning of the Decalogue: 'There shall be no strange god among you; you shall not bow down to a foreign god. I am the Lord your God, who brought you up out of the land of Egypt.' These words clearly reflect the beginning of the Decalogue, 'I am the Lord your God, who brought you out of the land of Egypt, out of the house of bondage. You shall have no other gods before me.' Another psalm which is clearly a covenant renewal psalm is Psalm 50. That this is pre-exilic is suggested by the evident citation of v. 2 in Lam. 2.15, 'All who pass along the way clap their hands at you; they hiss and wag their heads at the daughter of Jerusalem: "Is this the city which was called the perfection of beauty, the joy of all the earth?" (The expression 'the joy of all the earth' is in turn a quotation from Ps. 48.2.)

Psalm 50 seems to represent a cultic re-enactment of the Sinai pericope in Exodus 19; 20; 24. The following parallels are significant and serve to justify this statement:

Exod. 19.16-20 Yahweh's theophany in thunder and lightning	Cf. Ps. 50.3 '... before him is a devouring fire, round about him a mighty tempest'.
Exod. 20.1-17 The Decalogue	Cf. Ps. 50.16-20 The seventh, eighth, and ninth commandments.
Exod. 24.3-8 Ratification of the covenant by sacrifice	Cf. Ps. 50.5 'Gather to me my faithful ones, who made a covenant with me by sacrifice'.

A good case can therefore be made out that Psalm 50 represents a cultic re-enactment of the events reported in the Sinai pericope in Exodus 19–24, and as we have seen, there are good grounds for associating this with Tabernacles.

However, a number of cautionary remarks need to be added. First it should be observed that whereas Weiser thought in terms of a yearly ceremony of covenant renewal, Deut. 31.9ff. implies a seven-yearly ceremony. If there had previously been a yearly ceremony of covenant renewal, the change to a seven-yearly ceremony would have led to a reduction of emphasis on covenant, which runs counter to the purpose of the book of Deuteronomy. (Mowinckel, however, thought that it was because Deuteronomy was so long that its reading was restricted to every seven years.) Perhaps, as E. Kutsch argued, we should think of a seven-yearly covenant renewal ceremony.

A second cautionary note is that the Tabernacles covenant renewal ceremony may well only relate to a limited period in the late pre-exilic period. In recent years the view has been strongly questioned that covenant as a way of envisaging Yahweh's relation with Israel goes all the way back to Moses. Some scholars such as L. Perlitt argue that covenant theology was an invention of the Deuteronomists in the seventh century BC. This, however, is rather extreme, since there are references to the covenant already in the preaching of the eighth century prophet Hosea (Hos. 6.7; 8.1). Deuteronomistic covenant theology therefore represents an elaboration and emphasizing of something that goes back at least to the time of Hosea, and probably earlier. If there was a covenant renewal ceremony at Tabernacles encompassing Psalms 50 and 81 in pre-exilic Israel, it may well have functioned in the latter part of the monarchical period. It is interesting that Psalm 50 follows the earlier covenant pattern of JE (the Yahwistic and Elohistic sources found in Exodus 19–24), rather than that of Deuteronomy, so it should be pre-621 BC.

A third cautionary note is that in the post-exilic period covenant renewal seems to have been associated with the feast of Weeks (Pentecost) rather than Tabernacles. This is reflected in the dates given in the late Priestly source of the Pentateuch (cf. Exod. 19.1) and also in the book of *Jubilees*, and in a covenant renewal festival at Qumran, which was held at this time. The feast of Weeks has been associated with covenant and the Law also in Judaism subsequently.

The Role of the King at the Autumn Festival

This will be dealt with in the next chapter on royal psalms. For a positive estimation of this see the section on Psalm 132 (under 'Other psalms for special occasions') in Chapter 6; and for a critique of two questionable views see the concluding sections on 'The King as a God—the Myth and Ritual School' and especially 'The theory of a ritual humiliation of the king'.

Further Reading

For Mowinckel's classic presentation of the Autumn festival as one of Yahweh's enthronement:

S. Mowinckel, *Psalmenstudien*, 2.
S. Mowinckel, *The Psalms in Israel's Worship*, 1, 106-92, and
    the notes in 2, 222-50, where he replies to critics.

In broad agreement with Mowinckel:

J. Day, *God's Conflict with the Dragon and the Sea: Echoes of a Canaanite Myth in the Old Testament*, ch. 1, esp. 18-21, 35-37.

J. Gray, *The Biblical Doctrine of the Reign of God*, Edinburgh: T. & T. Clark, 1979, 7-71.

B. Halpern, *The Constitution of the Monarchy in Israel* (Harvard Semitic Monographs, 25), Chico: Scholars, 1981, 51-109.

E. Lipiński, *La Royauté de Yahwé dans la poésie et le culte de l'ancien Israël*, 2nd edn, Brussels: Palais der Acadamiën, 1968.

T.N.D. Mettinger, *In Search of God: The Meaning and Message of the Everlasting Names*, Philadelphia: Fortress, 1987, 92-122.

Works associating the Feast of Tabernacles with Yahweh's kingship but not enthronement:

Jörg Jeremias, *Das Königtum Gottes in den Psalmen* (FRLANT, 141), Göttingen: Vandenhoeck & Ruprecht, 1987.

A.R. Johnson, *Sacral Kingship in Ancient Israel*, 2nd edn, Cardiff: University of Wales Press, 1967.

H.-J. Kraus, *Psalms 1–59*, 86-89. (However, Kraus saw Tabernacles primarily as a Royal-Zion festival. See above, and chapter 6.)

B.C. Ollenburger, *Zion, the City of the Great King: A Theological Symbol of the Jerusalem Cult* (JSOT Supplement Series, 41), Sheffield: JSOT, 1987, 23-52.

Works rejecting the concept of the Autumn Festival as one of either Yahweh's kingship or enthronement:

S. Aalen, *Die Begriffe 'Licht' und 'Finsternis' im Alten Testament, im Spätjudentum und im Rabbinismus* (Skrifter utgitt av det Norske Videnskape-Akademi i Oslo. II. Hist-Filos. Kl., 1951, no. 1), Oslo: Dybwad, 1951, 60-63.

D.J.A. Clines, 'New Year', in *The Interpreter's Dictionary of the Bible, Supplementary Volume*, Nashville: Abingdon, 1976, 627-28.

N.H. Snaith, *The Jewish New Year Festival*, London: SPCK, 1947, 195-203.

R. de Vaux, *Ancient Israel*, 2nd edn, London: Darton, Longman & Todd, 1965, 504-506.

The following works in German are also relevant to the translation of *Yahweh mālak* and the interpretation of the Enthronement psalms:

H. Gunkel, *Einleitung in die Psalmen*, 94-116.

L. Köhler, 'Syntactica III. IV. Jahwäh mālāk', *VT* 3 (1953), 188-89.

H.-J. Kraus, *Die Königsherrschaft Gottes im Alten Testament* (Beiträge zur historischen Theologie, 13), Tübingen: Mohr, 1951.

O. Loretz, *Ugarit-Texte und Thronbesteigungspsalmen: Die Metamorphose des Regenspenders Baal–Jahwe (Ps 24,7-10; 29; 47; 93; 95–100 sowie Ps. 77,17-20; 114)* (Ugaritisch-Biblische Literatur, 7), Münster: Ugarit-Verlag, 1988.

D. Michel, 'Studien zu den sogenannten Thronbesteigungspsalmen', *VT* 6 (1956), 40-68.

J. Ridderbos, 'Jahwäh Malak', *VT* 4 (1954), 87-89.

J. Ulrichsen, 'Jhwh mālak', *VT* 27 (1977), 361-74.

P. Welten, 'Königsherrschaft Jahwes und Thronbesteigung. Bemerkungen zu unerledigten Fragen', *VT* 32 (1982), 297-310.

On the Autumn Festival as a Royal-Zion Festival:

H.-J. Kraus, *Worship in Israel*, Oxford: B. Blackwell, 1966, 183-88 (cf. 205-208).

On the Autumn Festival as one of Covenant Renewal:

S. Mowinckel, *Le Décalogue* (Etudes d'histoire et de philosophie religieuses, 16), Paris: Faculté de théologie protestante, Université de Strasbourg, 1927, 114-62.

A. Weiser, *The Psalms*, 35-52.

6

THE ROYAL PSALMS

How Many Royal Psalms?

TRADITIONALLY, OF COURSE, much of the Psalter was thought to be royal, inasmuch as the headings to the psalms in the Hebrew text attribute 73 of them to King David. However, there is no doubt that these headings are later additions to the text (see Chapter 7). For most modern scholars, the number of royal psalms is far fewer. H. Gunkel identified the royal psalms as Psalms 2; 18; 20; 21; 45; 72; 89; 101; 110; 132 and 144.1-11, and this oft-cited list may be taken as the irreducible minimum that would be accepted by almost all scholars. These psalms all make unambiguous reference to the king.

A few scholars, mostly Scandinavian and British, have argued for a very large number of royal psalms, and these scholars include Birkeland, the later Mowinckel, and more recently J.H. Eaton and S.J.L. Croft. However, they do not agree about the precise number of additional royal psalms which they envisage. Thus, Eaton regards as psalms with clearly royal content Psalms 3–4; 9/10; 17; 22–23; 27–28; 35; 40–41; 57; 59; 61–63; 66; 69–71; 75; 91–92; 94; 108; 118; 138; 140 and 143, and as less clear examples he cites Psalms 5; 11; 16; 31; 36; 42/3; 51–52 and 54. Again, Croft envisages the following psalms as royal in addition to Gunkel's irreducible minimum: Psalms 3; 5; 7; 9/10; 16–17; 22; 23; 26–28; 31; 38; 40; 44; 55–57; 59–63; 66; 69–71; 92; 94; 116; 118 and 138–143. Most of these additional royal psalms are individual laments, and in Chapter 2 we have already evaluated the arguments for considering such psalms as royal; we refer the reader back to there for details. We have conceded that more than

Gunkel's irreducible minimum could be royal. This seemed especially possible when the speaker appears to have a representative function on behalf of the nation, as when the enemies are clearly stated to be foreign nations (cf. Psalms 9/10; 56; 59). Even here, though, it is difficult to be certain, since other individuals could conceivably have played a representative role, as in Lamentations 3, where an individual appears to speak on behalf of Judah when there was no longer a king on the throne. Another individual lament where there is a plausible, though not certain, case for the subject's being a king is Ps. 3, where the psalmist's enemies are numbered at 'ten thousands of people' (v. 6). However, as we noted earlier, the language used in so many of the individual laments is of such a vague and general character that we can have little confidence that the subject must be a king, and they appear applicable to a wide number of individual situations of distress. Further, where we are given specific details, we find that the alleged martial imagery is often not really such, and that it is verbal rather than physical violence which is meant, as in Pss. 57.4 and 140.3, 9, which both Eaton and Croft claim as royal, or that the situation appears to be one of illness in which the psalmist is scolded by local Israelites, rather than one of war, as in Psalms 31, 35 and 69 (Eaton regards Psalms 35 and 69, and Croft Psalms 31 and 69, as royal).

Probably the weakest argument used by both Eaton and Croft for seeing psalms as royal is that of so-called royal style. For instance, to take examples from two non-lament psalms, it is by no means clear why a psalmist's referring to God as 'my shepherd' (Ps. 23.1) or 'my chosen portion and my cup' (Ps. 16.5) need imply that a king is speaking. It is clear from the Old Testament that many other persons besides the king saw themselves as standing in a close relationship to Yahweh, for example the prophets. In the case of Psalm 23, moreover, the verb used for anointing the head with oil (*dšn*) is not the one used everywhere else in connection with the anointing of kings (*mšḥ*), although both Eaton and Croft claim this to be another royal feature.

Another argument which Eaton and Croft employ as evidence of a large number of royal psalms is the heading *lᵉdāwîd* which is prefixed to approximately half the psalms in the Hebrew text. This clearly means 'By David' (see Chapter 7) and is generally regarded as evidence of an ascription of authorship applied to many of the psalms at a quite late period. Eaton and Croft do not deny that these psalms are not by David, but think that the heading may nevertheless provide evidence of a royal connection for these psalms. This, however, is a weak argument, since not only are the headings late but their clear meaning as an ascription of Davidic authorship would have to be reinterpreted. Further, both Eaton and Croft see a number of psalms which have this heading as non-royal, while others which lack it are nevertheless regarded as royal. The reliability of the heading as a royal indicator is therefore questionable.

The King in the Psalms as the Pre-exilic King

Traditionally royal psalms such as Psalms 2 and 110 have been given an eschatological messianic interpretation. Such an understanding is to be found in the New Testament (see Chapter 8); but the New Testament was itself building on the eschatological interpretation of these psalms within Judaism. Most modern scholars, however, since the rise of biblical criticism in the nineteenth century, have rejected this view, seeing the king here as an actually reigning Israelite monarch, admittedly spoken of in idealized language. The reason for this is that throughout the royal psalms the king is constantly spoken of as one who is already reigning, rather than as one whose arrival on the scene is expected in the future. Those advocating a purely eschatological understanding of the royal psalms tend now to be small in number, though they include a few French scholars such as R. Tournay. Another minority view held by a few nineteenth-century scholars, and revived recently by J. Becker and O. Loretz, maintains that these psalms in their final form are post-exilic compositions in which the 'king' is a mere collective symbol for the nation. (Nevertheless, Becker and Loretz often see authentic pre-exilic royal material underlying them.) However, this clearly conflicts with the natural reading of these psalms as relating to real individual kings.

At the end of the nineteenth and beginning of the twentieth century, when it was common to date most or all psalms late, the royal psalms were frequently thought to represent Maccabean or Hasmonean rulers of the second or first century BC. Apart from the unconventional Italian scholar M. Treves, this view now has no following; and most scholars today, rejecting this as well as the eschatological interpretation, understand the royal psalms as referring to Israelite kings of the pre-exilic period. Among the arguments supporting such a view are the following. First, there is now general agreement that the Psalter was finalized before the Maccabean era. (Cf. for instance 1 Chron. 16.36, from the fourth century BC, which already cites Psalm 106 along with its concluding editorial doxology [v. 48].) The only previous Israelite kings were those of the pre-exilic era. Secondly, the divine name Yahweh is freely used in the royal psalms; by the time of the Hasmoneans, however, this had become rather rare owing to the sacredness with which the name Yahweh was viewed, so that alternatives had to be found. Thirdly, Ps. 110.4 speaks of the king as a 'priest for ever after the order of Melchizedek', i.e. the pre-Israelite Jebusite priest-king of Salem (Jerusalem) in Genesis 14, and such a fusion with the Jebusite king ideology is most readily explicable soon after David's conquest of Jerusalem. Fourthly, Psalm 132 implies the existence of the Ark (v. 8), which no longer existed after 586 BC.

The Various Types of Royal Psalm

As with certain other types of psalm, the designation 'royal psalms' is not strictly a form-critical category, since there is no typical structure which characterizes them, and various forms may be found within them, for example individual thanksgiving (Psalm 18) or lament (Psalm 89). Rather what we have here is a classification on the basis of content. Various situations are presupposed in the royal psalms, and these will now be considered.

Coronation Psalms (Psalms 2 and 110)

Within the Psalter there are two psalms which are generally
accepted to be coronation psalms, Psalms 2 and 110. (Psalms
72 and 101 may also belong to this context—see below.) Their
coronation setting is suggested by the divine oracles which
they contain for the king: Ps. 2.7, 'I will tell of the decree of the
Lord: He said to me, "You are my son, today I have begotten
you"', and Ps. 110.1, 4, 'The Lord says to my lord: "Sit at my
right hand, till I make your enemies your footstool."... The
Lord has sworn and will not change his mind, "You are a
priest for ever after the order of Melchizedek"'.

In the books of Kings we are given some idea of the proce-
dure adopted in the coronation of Israelite kings in the cases of
Solomon (1 Kgs 1.33f.) and Joash (2 Kgs 11). These indicate
that the ceremony consisted of two main parts, the anointing
in the sanctuary and the enthronement in the king's palace.
Some points of contact between the coronation psalms and the
accounts in Kings may be noted. First, 2 Kgs 11.12 states in
connection with Joash's coronation that Jehoiada the priest
'put the crown upon him, and gave him the testimony *('ēdût)'*.
What is meant by the testimony is not completely certain, but
it is most likely to be connected with the 'decree' (*ḥōq*) mentioned in Ps. 2.7ff., 'I will tell of the decree of the Lord: He said
to me, "You are my son, today I have begotten you. Ask of me,
and I will make the nations your heritage, and the ends of the
earth your possession. You may break them with a rod of iron,
and dash them in pieces like a potter's vessel."' It seems that
we have here an allusion to the document containing Yahweh's promise to the king embodied in the Davidic covenant.
Another point of contact between the coronation psalms and
the accounts in Kings concerns Ps. 110.7, where we read of the
king, 'He will drink from the brook by the way, therefore he
will lift up his head'. There may be some allusion here to the
Gihon spring, at which Solomon was anointed king according
to 1 Kgs 1.33f., 38f.

A Royal Marriage Psalm (Psalm 45)

Psalm 45 is unique in the Psalter in that it is a royal marriage psalm. The royal bridegroom is described in vv. 2-9 and the bride in vv. 10-15. There can be no doubt that the psalm was intended for the marriage of an Israelite king. The traditional messianic interpretation, which understood the king as the coming Messiah and the bride as Israel, is inappropriate, since the bridegroom and bride are spoken of as already present, and there is nothing to suggest that the latter is merely an allegorical symbol. However, this was doubtless the interpretation of the psalm put upon it by its canonizers (cf. the Aramaic Targum, Hebrews 1.8f., and in our own day, still a few Catholic scholars like R. Tournay). The view of G. Widengren and others that the psalm depicts a sacred marriage is also uncalled for, as is T.H. Gaster's claim that the 'king' and 'queen' are mere symbols of ordinary Israelites, as is sometimes supposed to be the case in the Song of Songs. (It is far more likely that the Song of Songs is a post-exilic depiction of the love between Solomon and one of his foreign wives.)

Most modern scholars rightly accept that the psalm depicts the marriage of an Israelite king. It is impossible to relate it to any specific king; indeed, it was doubtless employed regularly in royal marriage ceremonies. The view that it is a northern psalm in origin is based on a misunderstanding of v. 12, for 'the daughter of Tyre' referred to there seems to be not the bride of the king (which might suggest Ahab or some other northern king); the phrase rather alludes to the people of Tyre (on analogy with such expressions as 'daughter of Zion'). For the disputed question whether the king is called a god in v. 6, see below.

Royal Battle Psalms (Psalms 18, 20, 89, 144, etc.)

The king was the head of the armed forces; and in the ancient world divine aid was expected in battle. Accordingly, it is not surprising to find that a number of royal psalms have a battle context. Psalms 20 and 144 are prayers to Yahweh appealing for aid prior to war, and if such individual lament psalms as 3, 9/10, 56 and 59 are also royal, this would be the context for them too. (Compare the large number of enemies in Ps. 3.6, and the identification of the enemies as foreigners in Pss. 9.5, 8, 15, 17, 19; 10.16; 56.7; 59.5, 8, which give some credence to the royal interpretation of these particular psalms.) The language employed in these psalms is sufficiently vague and general to suggest that they were repeatedly used in war situations and probably do not reflect particular historical events. Interestingly, 2 Chronicles 20 actually depicts the kind of setting these psalms would have had, for we read there that, faced with an invasion of Moabites, Ammonites and Meunites, King Jehoshaphat called a fast; and in vv. 6-12 we have the prayer to Yahweh for deliverance which he offered in the Jerusalem temple.

Rather surprisingly, a text bearing some relation to Psalm 20 has been found written in the Aramaic language but in Egyptian demotic script: the Amherst papyrus 63. This demotic Aramaic text has been variously dated to the second or fourth centuries BC and appears to be a paganized version of Psalm 20. However, the royal elements are missing from the demotic Aramaic text. Loretz has attempted to maintain that it is the biblical psalm which is dependent on the Aramaic text; and he regards the apparently royal elements as post-exilic additions in which the nation of Israel is symbolized as a king, just as he regards certain other of the so-called royal psalms as being really collective psalms. This, however, is most improbable. Psalm 20 is most naturally understood as relating to a pre-exilic Israelite king.

A psalm which appears to be a king's thanksgiving for victory in war is Psalm 18, a variant of which also appears in 2 Samuel 22. In both cases the superscription ascribes the psalm to David 'on the day when the Lord delivered him from the hand of all his enemies, and from the hand of Saul'. However, it is widely agreed that this is evidence of the later interpretation of the psalm rather than its original meaning, since it lacks the concrete, precise details that would warrant such a setting. This interpretation does, however, go back to at least the late seventh or sixth century BC, in view of its presence in 2 Sam. 22.1 as part of the deuteronomistic history, and a number of scholars claim that the psalm is an ancient one on the basis of its language. The vagueness of the language suggests that it was used repeatedly in situations of war. (For the theory of its employment at a ritual humiliation of the king at the feast of Tabernacles, see below.) The psalm has a number of similarities to the royal lament psalm Psalm 144 mentioned above, and may well have influenced it.

Psalm 89 may be divided into three main sections. The first part (vv. 1-18) is hymnic in nature, extolling Yahweh's covenant promise to David, his power in creation, and so on. The second part (vv. 19-37) alludes at some length to a divine oracle (presumably the oracle of Nathan, 2 Sam. 7) in which the promise is made to David that his descendants would rule for ever, although allowance is made for limited divine chastisements if disobedience occurred. The third section (vv. 38-51) is a painful lament, in which Yahweh is accused of having broken his promise to David, for the king has been overthrown in battle and apparently killed, and a prayer for Yahweh's intervention and deliverance is poured forth. Although some have supposed this psalm to be made up of two or three independent poems, in its present form it is certainly a well constructed, unified whole. It seems most likely that it dates from the time of the Babylonian exile in the sixth century BC, for this would cohere with the feeling of finality and utter rejection of the Davidic covenant that the psalm conveys, though the death of King Josiah in battle in 609 BC and the deportation of King Jehoiachin in 597 BC have also been suggested as possible occasions. Psalm 89 seems to be related to the ending of the Davidic monarchy in 586 BC in the same way that Psalms 74 and 79 are to the destruction of the Jerusalem temple of the same year. (See below for a critique of the view that Psalm 89 depicts a ritual humiliation of the king.)

Other Psalms for Special Occasions
(Psalms 101, 72, 21, 132)

Psalm 101 sets out the high ideal that should characterize the king's rule. That the subject is the king seems clear from v. 8. There is some dispute whether the psalm depicts the character of the rule that the king has been wont to exercise or whether it represents an oath outlining the intended nature of the king's future rule. The imperfect or future tense of the verbs suggests the latter. As such it is appropriate to the coro-

nation service, though conceivably it was uttered at other
times too. The lament rhythm of the psalm (the *qînâ* metre)
and the king's plea to God in v. 2, 'Oh when wilt thou come to
me?', may indicate that the psalm constitutes the oath of the
king made during the course of a penitential rite at the time of
his coronation and possibly renewed at the feast of Tabernacles. The negative confession uttered by the Babylonian king
during the course of the Babylonian New Year festival is a
possible though not a certain analogy. (For a critique of the
theory that Psalm 101 had its setting in a ritual battle, see
below.)

Psalm 72 sets out an idealized picture of the king's rule, concentrating on his provision of social justice for the poor and
oppressed, the universal extent of his dominion, and the general ethos of prosperity and well-being that prevails. Conceivably it had its setting at the coronation ceremony.

Psalm 21 is a royal psalm whose life setting is not entirely
clear. It has often been interpreted as a psalm of thanksgiving
for victory in battle. However, while vv. 1-7 have something of
the character of thanksgiving, the content seems rather vague
and general and there is no reference to battle, and vv. 8-13
imply victory over enemies as something still to occur in the
future. Hence, some scholars have understood Psalm 21 as a
psalm recited *before* battle, like Psalm 20; but this too seems
unsatisfactory in the light of the first half of the psalm. Verse 3
refers to the setting of a crown of fine gold on the head of the
king, which has led others to see this as a coronation psalm. On
the other hand, the rest of the psalm does not particularly suggest a coronation context. Possibly the psalm was sung at the
anniversary of the king's coronation.

Psalm 132 is a very interesting psalm in that it centres on
two main themes which occur also in 2 Samuel 6–7. In 2
Samuel 6 we read of David's bringing the Ark of the Covenant,
the symbol of Yahweh's presence, up into Jerusalem, and this
event is recalled in Ps. 132.1-10, while the consequent divine
presence in Zion is reaffirmed in vv. 13-16. 2 Samuel 7 contains the important divine oracle delivered by the prophet
Nathan stating that David's descendants would rule for ever,
though obedience on their part is necessary. This Davidic
covenant is recalled in Ps. 132.11-12, 17-18. It would appear

that Psalm 132 envisages the cultic re-enactment of these two important elements of the pre-exilic royal Zion faith. Since Solomon brought the Ark up into the temple at the time of the feast of Tabernacles in 1 Kings 8, and since there is evidence elsewhere in the Psalter of a connection between a procession with the Ark and Yahweh's kingship, which latter was associated with the feast of Tabernacles (see above, chapter 5), there are grounds for believing that Psalm 132 reflects cultic elements of the feast of Tabernacles. In the Chronicler's version of the events of 1 Kings 8, part of Psalm 132 is actually quoted (2 Chron. 6.41-42; cf. Ps. 132.8-10).

The Religious Role of the King in the Psalms

An idealized picture

As has already been stated, though originally relating to pre-exilic Israelite monarchs, the royal psalms depict the king in idealized language, e.g. he is promised universal rule and reigns with complete justice and righteousness. This reflects the traditional court style of the ancient near east and is attested also in Egypt and Mesopotamia. Clearly a kingly ideal is being set forth here that was not achieved in reality. One may compare the wish expressed at British coronation services, 'Long live the king! May the king live for ever!' It was the fact that the Israelite kings as a whole failed to live up to the ideal expressed in the psalms that led to the eschatologization of the imagery. Clearly this was the case after the exile, when there was no longer a Davidic king on the throne in whom the hopes expressed in the psalms could be invested, but it may be the case that some Israelites, at least, already envisaged an ideal future ruler before the exile: Isa. 9.2-7 may reflect this, unless it refers to an actual Israelite king such as Hezekiah. The imagery used of the future Messiah can be traced point after point back to the royal ideology of the psalms, e.g. the picture of the Messiah ruling justly and righteously (Isa. 11.3-5; cf. Ps. 72.1-4), reigning over the whole world (Zech. 9.10; cf. Ps. 72.8-11), and descended from David (Mic. 5.2; cf. Ps. 89.49).

We shall now consider certain terms employed in the
Psalter to describe the religious status of the king.

The Lord's Anointed

In post-biblical and Christian usage the term Messiah has
come to be used of the eschatological king. The word means
'Anointed (one)', the Greek rendering of which is *Christos*,
whence our word Christ. However, while the Old Testament
knows the idea of a coming eschatological king, the term
Messiah (Hebrew *māšîaḥ*) is never used of this figure there,
though this expression was, of course, subsequently used by the
Jews with this meaning. Nevertheless, the term is found in the
psalms, and there it is clearly used of the current reigning
king of the Davidic line (cf. Pss. 2.2; 18.50 = 2 Sam. 22.51; 20.6;
89.38, 51; 132.10, 17).

It seems that this expression is used with reference to the
fact that the king was anointed with oil at the time of his coronation. The Old Testament has a number of references to the
anointing of Israelite kings, e.g. Saul, David and Solomon (1
Sam. 10.1; 16.3; 1 Kgs 1.39), and in connection with David we
hear that the Spirit of Yahweh came upon him at the time of
his anointing (1 Sam. 6.13). It seems that anointing was an act
of consecration, setting the king aside as a sacred person (cf. 1
Sam. 24.6; 26.11). This is made explicit in the references to the
anointing of the high priests in the post-exilic period (cf. Lev.
8.12). It is very likely that this was one of a number of points
where the post-exilic high priests had inherited features previously associated with the pre-exilic monarchy, another being
the head-dress.

E. Kutsch, however, claims that the Israelite kings were
called 'the Lord's anointed' in a transferred sense, like the
Persian king Cyrus in Isa. 45.1, rather than in virtue of their
actual anointing with oil. However, with regard to the term
'the Lord's Anointed', this is more readily comprehensible if it
were the extension of a literal sense, although Isa. 45.1 is probably using it in a transferred sense. Moreover, the fact that
Kutsch accepts that kings were anointed at their coronation
makes it more natural to suppose that allusions to 'the Lord's
Anointed' refer back to this act.

It seems most probable that Israel adopted anointing from the surrounding Canaanites, who had had a tradition of many city-state kingships. Jotham's fable implies Canaanite anointing of kings in Judg. 9.8, 15, and preparation of unguents for the anointing of the Canaanite god Baal's would-be successor Athtar is probably alluded to in the Ugaritic texts (cf. J.A. Emerton, 'Ugaritic Notes', *JTS* 16 n.s. [1965], 441f.). The Canaanite practice of anointing kings has often been thought to be derived from either the Hittites or the Egyptians, the former of whom anointed their kings, while the latter anointed high officials and Syrian vassals. However, since we now know that royal anointing was already practised at Ebla in Syria in the third millennium BC, these hypotheses may well be unnecessary.

The King as God's Son

In Egypt, as we have noted earlier, the pharaoh was regarded as the son of the god Ra, i.e. he was really a god (the incarnation of Horus). Similarly, in the Canaanite world, at Ugarit, King Keret is regarded as the divine son of the god El. It is therefore interesting that in the psalms (and elsewhere in the Old Testament) the Israelite king is also called 'the son of God'. This terminology is clearly taken over from Israel's ancient near eastern environment, perhaps from Canaan.

The best known example is in Ps. 2.7, part of a psalm sung at the king's coronation. There the king declares, 'I will tell of the decree of the Lord: He said to me, "You are my son, today I have begotten you"'. There also appear to be cryptic allusions to the king's sonship in the other coronation psalm, Ps. 110.3. Again, more clearly, in Ps. 89.26-27, Yahweh declares of the Davidic king, 'He shall cry to me, "Thou art my Father, my God, and the Rock of my salvation". And I will make him the first-born, the highest of the kings of the earth.' This last passage echoes the oracle of Nathan to David in 2 Sam. 7.14, where Yahweh romises, 'I will be his father, and he shall be my son'.

However, although this terminology of the king as the son of God is taken up from Israel's ancient near eastern environment, it has clearly undergone a transformation. The king is no longer literally a god, but is rather understood as God's son by adoption. This is clear from the word 'today' in Ps. 2.7: the king is not son of God by nature, i.e. from the day of his birth, but rather because God so decides to regard him from the day of his coronation. Some scholars have questioned the applicability of the term 'adoption' here, but this does seem to be what is in mind. One may compare the Babylonian Laws of Hammurabi, where it is stipulated that when someone adopted a person, he said to him, 'You are my son'.

The king as a priest after the order of Melchizedek

In Ps. 110.4 we read the following words in connection with the king: 'The Lord has sworn and will not change his mind, "You are a priest for ever after the order of Melchizedek"'. This is the one place in the Psalter where the king is explicitly called a priest. The reference here must be to the king, since it is the king who is addressed elsewhere in the psalm. Moreover, Melchizedek is mentioned in Genesis 14 as the pre-Israelite Jebusite priest *and* king in Jerusalem (Salem), so it is clearly a royal priesthood that is being inherited. This means that we must reject H.H. Rowley's view that Ps. 110.4 is addressed to the priest (Zadok) rather than the Davidic king. We have evidence here of the fusion of the Jebusite and Israelite royal ideologies, and this is most naturally understood as having occurred soon after David's conquest of the Jebusite city of Jerusalem.

Some scholars have denied that the Israelite kings were regarded as priests, but this verse indicates unambiguously that they were. This coheres with other evidence from the historical books. Thus, in 2 Samuel 6, when King David brought up the Ark, the symbol of God's presence, into Jerusalem, we read that he 'was girded with a linen ephod'. The ephod, a kind of loincloth, was a specifically priestly garment (1 Sam. 22.18; cf. 1 Sam. 2.18; contrast the later more elaborate high priestly ephod in Exodus 28). On other occasions we hear of kings offering sacrifices—a specifically priestly role—and this is mentioned in connection with Saul, David, Solomon, Jeroboam and Ahaz (1 Sam. 13.9; 2 Sam. 6.17-19; 1 Kgs 3.4; 8.5, 62-64; 9.25; 13.1; 2 Kgs 16.12-16). It might be objected that in some instances this might mean no more than that the king had sacrifices offered, rather than offering them himself; but not all the texts cited are capable of this interpretation. Cf. 2 Kgs 16.12-13, where it is stated that 'the king drew near to the altar, and went up on it, and burned his burnt offering and his cereal offering, and poured his drink offering, and threw the blood of his peace offerings upon the altar'. We also find David and Solomon blessing the people in the sanctuary (2 Sam. 6.18; 1 Kgs 8.14), an act which is reserved to the priests according to Num. 6.22-27 and 1 Chron. 23.13. Finally, we see the king's headship over the state religion in the reforms of the cult undertaken, for example, by the kings Hezekiah and Josiah (2 Kgs 18.4; 23.1-25).

From all that we know, however, it seems clear that the king did not officiate as a priest every day in the sanctuary; rather this was the work of the ordinary priests. The king was clearly a king of a special type: he was a priest after the order of Melchizedek.

Two Questionable Views of the Religious Role of the King

The King as a God—the Myth and Ritual School

Both the so-called Myth and Ritual School centred on the British scholar S.H. Hooke—though he denied that it was a 'school'—and a number of Scandinavian scholars such a I. Engnell, G. Widengren, and G.W. Ahlström centred especially on Uppsala in Sweden, but not confined to it and likewise not strictly a 'school', put forward a number of views earlier this century about the role of the king in the cult, and especially in the feast of Tabernacles. These views were based on the assumption of a common ritual pattern throughout the countries of the ancient near east. Common to these scholars was the belief that the king in ancient Israel was thought of as literally a god; that he played the role of a god in the cult at the feast of Tabernacles (usually Yahweh, though Ahlström thought in terms rather of an assumed god called Dod); that the god was a dying and rising god, this sequence of events being ritually portrayed by the king; and that there was a sacred marriage between the god and goddess, also ritually enacted by the king.

The problem with these views is basically twofold: first, they have very little if any support in the biblical text itself, and secondly, the proposed common ancient near eastern ritual pattern is dubious. Consequently, they now have hardly any following among contemporary scholars. Thus, for example, with regard to the alleged common ritual pattern, it used to be widely believed that there was evidence for the death and resurrection of Marduk at the Babylonian New Year festival, but W. von Soden showed in 1955 that this was not so. Rather, the text to which appeal had been made had nothing to do with the New Year festival and was rather a piece of political propaganda. Also, it now emerges, according to W.G. Lambert, that the enactment of a sacred marriage at the Babylonian New Year festival is dubious.

With regard to kingship, it has been pointed out that we should differentiate carefully between the various cultures of the ancient near east. There was no one uniform pattern, as H. Frankfort pointed out in his book *Kingship and the Gods* (1948). The king in Egypt was indeed considered a god: son of Ra, incarnation of Horus, and assimilated to Osiris after his death. On the other hand, in Mesopotamia it was only until about 2000 BC that the kings were thought of as divine (symbolized by a horned head-dress). Amongst the Hittites the kings were deified after their death but not before. For the Canaanites there is evidence from the Ugaritic Keret epic that the king was considered a god, a son of the supreme god El. 'Do gods die?', Keret's son asks when his father is ill (cf. Gibson, 95).

However, in the Old Testament it is difficult to find any real evidence of the deification of the king. The king is clearly a human figure, Yahweh's servant. If the kings of Israel had really been thought of as divine, it is surprising that none of the Old Testament prophets ever criticized them on this score. The prophets often criticized Israelite kings for various misdemeanours but never for claiming to be divine. Foreign kings are, however, twice condemned for the hubris of their divine pretensions, namely in Isa. 14.12-15 and Ezek. 28.1ff. Moreover, the king of the northern kingdom of Israel explicitly denies divine status in 2 Kgs 5.7: 'Am I God (or a god), to kill and make alive, that this man sends word to me to cure a man of leprosy?'

Secondly, there is no trace in the Old Testament of any worship being offered to the king; rather, the people entreated God on behalf of the king (Pss. 20.1-5; 72.15). While it might be claimed that any trace of ruler worship would have been censored from the psalms, if there had been any ruler worship we should certainly expect it to be referred to in the historical books or the prophets, since they did not refrain from condemning Israel's manifold idolatries. Thirdly, as has been noted, the Israelite king was regarded as God's son *by adoption* (Ps. 2.7) from the time of his coronation, and so was not divine by nature.

There are good grounds, therefore, for maintaining that the Israelite king was not regarded as a god. There is, however, one verse in the psalms which might refer to the king as *ᵉlōhîm*, literally, 'god'. This comes in v. 6 of Psalm 45, a royal marriage psalm. On the most natural rendering of the Hebrew the king is there addressed in the words, 'Your throne, O God, is for ever and ever. Your royal sceptre is a sceptre of equity.' In fact, both the Greek Septuagint translation and, following it, Heb. 1.8 in the New Testament, understood *ᵉlōhîm* as a vocative here, 'O God', addressed to the king. How are we to make sense of this? There are two broad categories of interpretation of this verse, the first of which holds that the king is indeed here called 'god' (whether literally or hyperbolically), while the second gets round the problem by attempting to render the verse in some different way. We shall now consider the various possibilities.

In favour of the latter type of interpretation, it is claimed that the passage would be unique in the Old Testament if the king is here addressed as 'god'. It is pointed out that we could render the Hebrew as 'Your throne is like God's for ever and ever', on the understanding that the word for 'like' (*k*) has been omitted, perhaps for reasons of euphony, as the word translated 'your throne' (*kisᵉᵃkā*) already contains two *k*'s. A number of scholars, including C.R. North, have compared the Song of Songs, where in 1.15 the man says to the woman, 'your eyes are doves' (*ᵉênayik yônîm*), in contrast to 5.12, where the woman says of the man, 'his eyes are *like* doves (or doves' eyes)' (*'ēnāyw kᵉyônîm*). Alternatively, it has been suggested that one could render the passage in Psalm 45 as 'Your throne is God's for ever and ever', which would likewise avoid calling the king a god. Either of these renderings would correspond to the idea that we find in 1 Chron. 28.5, where Solomon is said 'to sit upon the throne of the kingdom of the Lord' (cf. 1 Chron. 29.23).

Though all this is possible, it must be admitted that the more natural way of taking *ᵉlōhîm* in Ps. 45.6 is as a vocative, hence 'Your throne, O God, is for ever and ever'. What further inclines one to this is the fact that in Isa. 9.6 the ideal eschatological king is similarly referred to as 'mighty god' (*'ēl gibbôr*). Some scholars avoid this conclusion by supposing that *'ēl gibbôr* might be rendered 'god of a hero', 'god' being understood as a superlative meaning 'mighty', hence 'mighty hero'. However, against this stands the fact that in all other instances of *'ēl gibbôr* or *hā'ēl haggibbôr* in the Old Testament the meaning is clearly '(the) mighty God' (Isa. 10.21; Deut. 10.17; Neh. 9.32; Jer. 32.18). Nevertheless, neither Ps. 45.6 nor Isa. 9.6 need be taken as implying that the king is literally thought of as a god, which would, as we have seen, appear to be contrary to the Old Testament view of the king. Possibly we have here examples of hyperbole or court style, which though deriving ultimately from Canaanite notions of divine kingship, were no longer taken literally. We should also bear in mind that the word *ᵉlōhîm* is used elsewhere in the Old Testament of beings who were not literally gods, but who doubtless had been regarded as such at an earlier stage, namely ghosts (1 Sam. 28.13; Isa. 8.19). Similarly, with the growth of absolute monotheism, when gods were demoted to the status of angels, they continued to be called *ᵉlōhîm*. The word in both Psalm 45 and Isaiah 9 may therefore have come to mean something like 'superhuman'. Interestingly, in both Psalm 45 and Isaiah 9 the context is that of the king as a warrior, something which scholars have hitherto not noticed. It may be, therefore, that Psalm 45, like Isaiah 9, has in mind in particular the king's superhuman power as a warrior.

In any case, whatever view we take of the controversial verse, it is clear that it is insufficient to bear the whole weight of the notion of divine kingship.

The Theory of a Ritual Humiliation of the King

A.R. Johnson, followed by J.H. Eaton and a number of Scandinavian scholars, posited an important role for the king in the Autumn festival (as did the Uppsala school), but without supposing that he was regarded as a god playing the role of a dying and rising Yahweh or engaging in a sacred marriage. Their position is more moderate and attempts to build on the evidence of the biblical text itself, rather than importing alien notions from outside Israel. It does, however, involve imaginative reconstruction in its postulation of ritual suffering and vindication of the king during the course of the festival.

Taking his stand on such psalms as Psalms 2; 18; 89; 101; 110 and 118, Johnson postulated a ritual drama in which the nations of the earth, who represented the forces of darkness and death opposed to Yahweh, united in an effort to destroy Yahweh's chosen people by slaying the Davidic king upon whom the people's survival depended. At first the king was allowed to suffer defeat and as a result was nearly engulfed in the waters of the underworld, but at the last moment, after a plea of loyalty to the Davidic covenant and an acknowledgment of his ultimate dependence upon Yahweh, he was delivered and restored to office. Thus, the prosperity of the nation, for which the king was directly responsible, was assured for another year.

Johnson's case is carefully argued. However, most scholars are sceptical of his reconstruction, since we have no unambiguous representation of the proposed ritual in any of the psalms, and it also possible to suggest alternative explanations of the psalms that have been brought into the discussion.

Thus Psalm 89 reads very much like the description of some important historical disaster that has overtaken the Davidic monarchy (very possibly the end of the southern kingdom in 586 BC), and there is no indication that imminent deliverance is on its way. This renders the explanation of the psalm as part of the ritual of royal suffering and vindication less likely.

Again, although Psalm 118 does portray a process of national
suffering and vindication, it is likely to be post-exilic (at any
rate in its present form), since v. 3 refers to 'the house of
Aaron', which makes best sense as a reference to the post-
exilic priests, who were known as 'the sons of Aaron' (in the
pre-exilic era the priests were the Levites). With regard to
Psalm 101, Johnson and his followers hold it to be an appeal by
the king on the basis of his ethical righteousness for deliverance by Yahweh during the course of the ritual battle. It is true
that the psalm is couched in the characteristic lament metre,
with which the words of v. 2 cohere, 'Oh when wilt thou come
to me?' However, it must be pointed out that the psalm makes
no reference to a battle, which would be surprising if this were
the intended context. Moreover, it should be noted that the
confession of innocence which the Babylonian king made
during the course of the New Year festival when his kingship
was renewed, which has been compared with Psalm 101, is
not set in a battle context. As for Psalms 2 and 110, neither of
these speak of the humiliation of the king. We are left with
Psalm 18, which certainly does depict a sequence of royal
humiliation and vindication, but it seems dangerous to recon-
struct an annual ritual ceremony on the basis of this when it
could very well be alluding to the situation of the king during
an actual battle.

Eaton has gone beyond Johnson in relating a number of
other psalms to the ritual battle in addition to those listed
above. One of these is Psalm 22, which had already been
assigned to this context by several Scandinavian scholars.
However, although the psalmist is in some kind of danger, it is
not at all clear that this is a battle, and there is no indication
that the enemies are foreigners. The psalm, whose subject
may well not be a king, does not seem, therefore, to belong to
the postulated context.

Further Reading

On the Royal Psalms generally:

K. Crim, *The Royal Psalms*, Richmond, VA.: John Knox, 1962.
S. Mowinckel, *The Psalms in Israel's Worship*, 1, 42-80.
L. Sabourin, *The Psalms: Their Origin and Meaning*, 2, 208-56.

Works envisaging a large number of Royal Psalms:

H. Birkeland, *The Evildoers in the Book of Psalms*.

S.J.L. Croft, *The Identity of the Individual in the Psalms*.

J.H. Eaton, *Kingship and the Psalms*.

S. Mowinckel, *The Psalms in Israel's Worship*, 1, 225-46.

For the more common view that the number of Royal Psalms is relatively small:

Most Psalm commentaries, e.g. A.A. Anderson, H.-J. Kraus.

W.H. Bellinger, *Psalmody and Prophecy*, 28-31.

H. Gunkel and J. Begrich, *Einleitung in die Psalmen*, 1, 140-76.

On the Coronation ritual:

K.A. Kitchen, *Ancient Orient and Old Testament*, London: Tyndale, 1966, 106-11 (criticisms of von Rad).

G. von Rad, 'The royal ritual in Judah', in *The Problem of the Hexateuch and Other Essays*, Edinburgh and London: Oliver and Boyd, 1965, 222-31.

R. de Vaux, *Ancient Israel*, 102-107.

Various aspects of the religious status of the King:

G. Cooke, 'The Israelite King as Son of God', *ZAW* 73 (1961), 202-25.

J.A. Emerton, 'The Syntactical Problem of Ps. 45.7', *JSS* 13 (1968), 58-63.

E. Kutsch, *Salbung als Rechtsakt im Alten Testament und im alten Orient* (BZAW, 87), Berlin: A. Töpelmann, 1963.

S. Mowinckel, *He that Cometh*, Oxford: B. Blackwell, 1959, 21-95.

C.R. North, 'The Religious Aspect of Hebrew Kingship', *ZAW* 50 (1932), 8-38.

J.R. Porter, 'Psalm XLV.7', *JTS* 12 (1961), 51-53.

H.H. Rowley, 'Melchizedek and Zadok (Gen 14 and Ps 110)', in W. Baumgartner *et al.* (eds.), *Festschrift Alfred Bertholet*, Tübingen: Mohr, 1950, 461-72.

On Ps. 89:

T. Veijola, *Verheissung in der Krise*, Helsinki: Suomalainen Tiedeakatemia, 1982.

For contrasting views on the relationship between Ps. 20 and the Amherst papyrus 63:

O. Loretz (with I. Kottsieper), *Die Königspsalmen: Die altorientalisch-kanaanäische Königstradition in jüdischer Sicht, 1—Ps 20, 21, 72, 101 und 144* (Ugaritisch-Biblische Literatur, 6), Münster: Ugarit-Verlag, 1988, 15-75.

C.F. Nims and R.C. Steiner, 'A Paganized Version of Psalm 20:2-6 from the Aramaic Text in Demotic Script', *JAOS* 103 (1983), 261-74.

For the 'Myth and Ritual' and Uppsala school view of a common pattern of kingship throughout the ancient Near East see:

I. Engnell, *Studies in Divine Kingship in the Ancient Near East*, Oxford: Blackwell, 1967.

S.H. Hooke (ed.), *Myth, Ritual and Kingship. Essays on the Theory and Practice of Kingship in the Ancient Near East and Israel*, Oxford: Clarendon, 1958. (See the essays by S.H. Hooke [1-21] and G. Widengren [149-203] for the more extreme positions with regard to Israel.)

For objections to these views see:

H. Frankfort, *Kingship and the Gods*, Chicago/London: University of Chicago Press, 1948.

M. Noth, 'God, King, and Nation in the Old Testament', in *The Laws in the Pentateuch and other essays*, Edinburgh/London: Oliver & Boyd, 1966, 144-78.

J.W. Rogerson, *Myth in Old Testament Interpretation* (BZAW, 134), Berlin/New York: de Gruyter, 1974, 66-84. (For criticisms of the 'Myth and Ritual' position more generally.)

On the theory of a ritual humiliation of the king:

Pro:

J.H. Eaton, *Kingship and the Psalms*. (Eaton also postulates royal atoning rites.)

A.R. Johnson, *Sacral Kingship in Ancient Israel*, 2nd edn, Cardiff: University of Wales Press, 1967.

Contra:

S.J.L. Croft, *The Identity of the Individual in the Psalms*, 85-88. (On 89-113 Croft presents an alternative reconstruction of the royal ritual.)

T.N.D. Mettinger, *King and Messiah: The Civil and Sacral Legitimation of the Israelite Kings* (Coniectanea Biblica, Old Testament Series, 8), Lund: C.W.K. Gleerup, 1976, 306-308.

Some idiosyncratic minority views dating the Royal Psalms to the postexilic period:

J. Becker, *Messianic Expectation in the Old Testament*, Edinburgh: T. & T. Clark, 1980.

O. Loretz (with I. Kottsieper), *Die Königspsalmen*.

7

THE COMPOSITION OF THE PSALTER

The Five-fold Division of the Psalter

THE PSALTER IS DIVIDED into five books: Psalms 1–41; 42–72; 73–89; 90–106 and 107–150. This is clearly a late editorial device and may have arisen in imitation of the five books of the Pentateuch. The first four books conclude with similar (though not identical) doxologies: Pss. 41.13; 72.18-19; 89.52; 106.48. The final psalm of book 5, and the last psalm of the whole Psalter, Psalm 150, lacks a doxology of this kind. However, this psalm is, in fact, one long doxology on the theme of 'Praise the Lord!'

It is interesting that 1 Chronicles 16's citation from Psalm 106 includes the doxology (v. 48) in v. 36: '"Blessed be the Lord, the God of Israel, from everlasting to everlasting!" All the people then said "Amen" and praised the Lord.' This may indicate that the Psalter had already been divided into books and was complete in the Chronicler's time in the fourth century BC.

The Deliberate Placing of Psalm 1

It is difficult not to believe that the placing of Psalm 1 at the very beginning of the Psalter represents a deliberate editorial intention (so B.S. Childs, G.H. Wilson). Its timeless message, holding before the reader the two ways—the way of the righteous and the way of the wicked—makes it appropriate as an introduction to the whole Psalter. However, G.H. Wilson is surely going too far when he states that Psalm 1's emphasis on meditating on the Law indicates that the Psalter in its final form is a book to be read rather than to be performed. This is a false antithesis, and is in any case contradicted by the musical superscriptions to the psalms.

Lectionary Theories of the Origin of the Ordering of the Psalms

Attempts have sometimes been made, e.g. by A. Arens, to explain the ordering of the psalms in the Psalter by supposing that it arose out of the lectionary needs of the synagogue. The psalms from the five books of the Psalter, it is claimed, would have been arranged for consecutive reading alongside consecutive passages (*sedarim*) from the five books of the Pentateuch (Torah) in a triennial cycle. However, this view is now generally discredited. Attempts to find parallels between the alleged corresponding pentateuchal and psalmic passages have proved to be forced, and the numbers of psalms and pentateuchal *sedarim* in each of the five books do not properly correspond. Moreover, it is now clear that the whole concept of a triennial reading of the Torah is a development belonging to the Christian era (cf. J. Heinemann) and so cannot possibly have influenced the arrangement of the Psalter.

The Theories of G.H. Wilson

G.H. Wilson, while accepting that many individual psalms have been arranged for reasons of supposed common authorship, genre, catchwords, etc.—reasons which we shall illustrate with examples below—also sees a larger, overarching purpose in the ordering of the Psalter as a whole. He finds it significant that royal psalms are found at a number of the 'seams' in books 1–3, i.e. Psalms 2; 72; 89; and he believes that Psalm 41 may also have functioned as a royal psalm. He thinks that books 1–2 celebrate Yahweh's covenant with David (cf. Psalms 2; 72), though by the end of book 3 the covenant has come to nothing (Psalm 89). Book 4 provides the answer to this problem with its message that Yahweh is king, that he has been Israel's refuge in the past, and that those who trust him are blessed. Book 4 ends with a plea for restoration from exile (Ps. 106.47), and book 5 is understood as providing an answer to this plea: trust in Yahweh.

It is difficult, however, to avoid the impression that this over-arching message claimed for the Psalter has been imposed on it by arbitrarily attaching special significance to particular psalms. Moreover, it is by no means clear that royal psalms have been consciously placed at the seams of the Psalter in books 1–3. Thus, on the one hand, Wilson offers no plausible explanation for the placing of non-royal psalms at the seams in Pss. 42/3 and 71, and (*pace* Wilson) there is no evidence that Ps. 41 ever functioned as royal (the Davidic heading is late). On the other hand, it needs to be recalled that from the point of view of the redactors a large number of the psalms were regarded as royal (cf. the Davidic superscriptions), so that it seems arbitrary to single out a few that modern scholarship would mostly understand as royal.

Reasons for the Ordering of the Psalms

It is apparent that any attempt to find one grandiose scheme to account for the ordering of the psalms is bound to end in fail-ure. On the other hand, careful study of the Psalter reveals that its arrangement is not *completely* haphazard and that a whole series of criteria have been operative. Sometimes the editors have put together psalms with the same superscrip-tion. On other occasions, it is possible to discern thematic rea-sons, common catchwords or genres which have led to par-ticular psalms being placed next to each other.

First, the explicit headings or superscriptions. Psalms 120–134 are all 'songs of the steps (or ascents)', Psalms 42/43–9; 84–85 and 87–88 are ascribed to the sons of Korah, Psalms 73–83 are attributed to Asaph (as also in Psalm 50, though this is separated from the others), and Psalms 3–9; 11–32; 34–41; 51–65; 68–70; 108–110, and 138–145 are said to be by David (as also are Psalms 86; 101; 103; 122; 124; 131 and 133, though these stand isolated). Within the Davidic group Psalms 52–55 are entitled 'A Maskil of David' and Psalms 56–60 'A Miktam of David'. Also Psalms 42/43–45 are headed 'A Maskil of the sons of Korah' and Psalms 88–89 'A Maskil of Ethan the Ezrahite'.

As for other criteria of arrangement, we find for example that Psalms 104–106; 111–113; 115–117; and 146–150 all

begin or end (or both!) with *Hallelujah*, 'Praise the Lord'.
Within the group Psalms 104–106, both Psalms 105 and 106
have in common a detailed historical retrospect, and then
Psalm 104 has in common with Psalm 103 the fact it begins
'Bless the Lord, O my soul' (Psalm 103 also ends with these
words). Again, Ps. 106.47 reads, 'Save us, O Lord our God, and
gather us from among the nations' and Ps. 107.3 similarly has
'and [the Lord] gathered us in from the lands', which thus
serves to bind them together.

Psalms 93; 96–99 are all enthronement psalms. Psalm 95 is
also concerned with Yahweh's kingship, and Psalm 94 with its
emphasis on Yahweh as judge of the earth also fits in quite well
in this sequence of psalms. In addition, Ps. 100.3 parallels Ps.
95.7 with its words 'we are his people and the sheep of his
pasture'. One of the enthronement psalms, Psalm 47, is admittedly separated from the rest, but it has nevertheless been
placed in a thematically appropriate place between Psalms 46
and 48, which are both concerned with the inviolability of Zion.
The twin themes of Yahweh's kingship and the inviolability of
Zion are also found together in both Isaiah 33 and Zechariah
14, which indicates that they are indeed closely related.

Other examples of psalms with related themes are Psalms
50 and 51, which have similar critical statements about
sacrifice, and Psalms 135 and 136, which have both verbal and
thematic parallels in their references to the Exodus and conquest (regarding Sihon, king of the Amorites, and Og, king of
Bashan). The catchword principle provides a connection
between the last verse of Psalm 32 and first verse of Psalm 33.

A considerable number of the individual laments come
together in groups: Psalms 3–7; 25–28; 38–40 (at any rate the
first half of Psalm 40); 54–57; 69–71; and 140–143. Within
Psalms 38–40, Psalms 38 and 39 are clearly psalms of illness,
and so is Psalm 41, which is in form an individual thanksgiving psalm rather than a lament, so one wonders whether
Psalm 40 may not have been understood as an illness psalm
too. Again, Psalms 65–66 are thanksgiving psalms, and
Psalms 20–21 are both royal psalms. Doubtless a careful student would discover even more connecting links between the
psalms than those mentioned here.

Finally, in so far as there is an overall pattern in the arrangement of the psalms, it is surely in terms of a movement from lamentation to praise, since laments greatly predominate in the first half of the Psalter and hymns in the second half. However, this is only a general tendency and not a rigid rule.

Evidence of Earlier Collections and the Elohistic Psalter

There is clear evidence that the collecting together of the psalms did not all take place at once. Various pointers indicate that earlier collections were made that have subsequently been joined together in our Psalter. Thus, in Ps. 72.20, at the end of book 3, we are informed that 'The prayers of David, the son of Jesse, are ended', although in our current Psalter the headings of numerous subsequent psalms declare that they too are by David (Psalms 86; 101; 103; 108–110; 122; 124; 131; 133; 138–145). This makes sense only if books 1–2 had originally constituted a separate collection from books 3–5. Again, we find that a number of psalms are duplicated: Psalm 14 = Psalm 53, Ps. 40.13-17 = Psalm 70, and Psalm 108 = Pss. 57.7-11 + 60.5-12. This too is more readily explicable if the duplicates had originally belonged to different collections.

One clear piece of earlier editing is apparent within Psalms 42–83, commonly known as the Elohistic Psalter. This appellation derives from the fact that, uniquely within the Psalter, the word Elohim (English Bibles: 'God') occurs here far more frequently than the name Yahweh (English Bibles: 'the Lord'). Thus, whereas in Pss. 1–41 we find 272 instances of Yahweh (or 278 if we include the headings and doxology) and 15 instances of Elohim, in Psalms 84–89 31 occurrences of Yahweh and 7 of Elohim, and within Psalms 90–150 339 appearances of Yahweh and 6 of Elohim, the situation is reversed in Psalms 42–83, for there Yahweh is found only 43 times (excluding the doxology in Ps. 72.18) but Elohim a full 200 times. That this situation is to be explained by editorial activity whereby the name Elohim has been systematically (though not universally) substituted for Yahweh is clear from a number of indications. Thus, first, there are instances within these psalms where the occurrence of Elohim reads oddly, as in Ps.

50.7, 'I am God, your God' and Ps. 45.7 'Therefore, God, your
God, has anointed you'; in both cases 'the Lord, your God'
would read more smoothly. Secondly, where passages from
the Elohistic Psalter occur elsewhere in the Old Testament we
find Yahweh standing instead of Elohim. The parallel can
occur outside the Psalter altogether, as in Ps. 68.1, 7, 8, which
quote Num. 10.35; Judg. 5.4, 5, or within the Psalter itself as in
the case of the duplicate psalms, Psalm 14 = Psalm 53 and Ps.
40.13-17 = Psalm 70 (though curiously, in Ps. 70.5, Yahweh
occurs instead of the Elohim of Ps. 40.17). The fact that the
parallel to Ps. 57.7-11 + Ps. 60.5-12 in Psalm 108 likewise uses
Elohim is no problem, since it is clear that Psalm 108 has
appropriated its verses from the Elohistic Psalter; this is
apparent from the situation that (apart from Ps. 144.9) Psalm
108 contains the only instances of Elohim within the whole of
Psalms 90–150.

At an earlier stage too various collections of psalms were
made that have subsequently been incorporated into our
Psalter. These include the psalms attributed to David (Psalms
3–9; 11–32; 34–41; 51–65; 68–70; 86; 101; 103; 108–110; 122;
124; 131; 133; 138–145); the psalms associated with the temple
musicians Asaph (Psalms 50; 73–83) and the sons of Korah
(Psalms 42–49; 84–85; 87–88); and the so-called songs of the
steps (or ascents) (Psalms 120–134).

The Psalms of David

The psalms attributed to David in the headings in Hebrew are
Psalms 3–9; 11–32; 34–41; 51–65; 68–70; 86; 101; 103; 108–
110; 122; 124; 131; 133; and 138–145, approximately half the
Psalter. It has sometimes been claimed that *lᵉdāwîd* in these
headings does not mean 'by David' but rather 'concerning
David', being comparable to such expressions in the Ugaritic
texts as *lb'l* 'concerning Baal'. However, this view is difficult to
sustain. We may take, for instance, the superscription to
Psalm 7, 'A Shiggaion *lᵉdāwîd*, which he sang to the Lord
concerning Cush a Benjaminite', or Psalm 18, 'A psalm
lᵉdāwîd the servant of the Lord, who addressed the words of
this song to the Lord on the day when the Lord delivered him
from the hand of Saul. He said: ... ' It is impossible to suppose

that *lᵉdāwîd* in these instances is anything but an ascription of authorship.

There is now general agreement that these headings should not be taken as factually authentic. Although some psalms may be as old as the time of David (e.g. Psalm 110), it would be a bold scholar who could claim any particular psalms to be by him (but cf. now M.D. Goulder). Sometimes the headings specify particular events in David's life as the occasion for the psalm in question (Psalms 3; 7; 18; 34; 51–52; 54; 56–57; 59–60; 63; 142), usually referring to episodes known from the books of Samuel. However, there is no doubt that these headings are later additions to the text, since they hardly ever match the actual contents of the psalm in more than a very general way, and sometimes they are quite inappropriate. They thus provide evidence of the history of interpretation of the psalms, rather than of their original setting. The increasing tendency to ascribe more and more psalms to David is illustrated by the Greek Septuagint, where the number rises from 73 to 85 (including the additional Psalm 151), sometimes with further precise details of circumstances.

Although most of these psalms are not even royal, let alone by David, it is quite likely that a large number of them derive from the pre-exilic period, when the Davidic monarchy ruled. They are especially concentrated in books 1–2 of the Psalter, which appear to contain many of the earliest psalms, those dating from before the exile.

The Psalms of the Sons of Korah

The following psalms have headings which associate them with the sons of Korah: Psalms 42–49; 84–85; and 87–88 (Psalm 88 is also attributed to Heman the Ezrahite). Of these Psalms 42/43; 46; 48; 84; and 87 are especially concerned with Mt Zion, and their strong emphasis in its inviolability (cf. Psalms 46; 48) suggests a pre-exilic origin before the first temple was destroyed (*contra* G. Wanke). There are no good reasons for disputing an origin in Jerusalem, which their pervasive Zion theology suggests. This has not, however, prevented two scholars from suggesting quite different origins. Thus, J. Maxwell Miller sees the Korahite psalms as originating from southern Judah, while M.D. Goulder (who does not discuss Miller's suggestion) views them as having originated at the other end of Israel at the sanctuary of Dan in the Northern Kingdom, specifically in the Autumn festival.

Miller's arguments start from the fact that reference is made to the *bny qrḥ* 'sons of Korah' on an ostracon found near the sanctuary at Arad in southern Judah (cf. Y. Aharoni, *Arad Inscriptions*, no. 49, line 2). This may or may not refer to the levitical sons of Korah of the Bible, but even if it does, it cannot be gainsaid that there are no clear references to southern Judah in these psalms, whereas allusions to Zion are all-pervasive. Miller thinks that the reference in Ps. 48.2 to Mt Zion's being 'in the far north' supports his view of the southern vantage-point of these psalms. However, it is far more likely that the phrase in question is a mythical one, to be rendered 'in the heights of Zaphon'. Zaphon was the name of Baal's mountain-dwelling in the Ugaritic texts and is associated with the divine name Elyon ('the Most High') in Isa. 14.13-14, El-'Elyon ('God Most High') being the name of the Jebusite deity of *Jerusalem*, equated by the Israelites with Yahweh (cf. Gen. 14.18-20, 22). The Jerusalemite divine name Elyon is actually employed in the related Korahite psalm, Ps. 46.4, and there are other clear mythical allusions of a distinctly Jerusalemite character in both Psalms 46 and 48. In Ps. 46.4 we find the mythical 'river whose streams make glad the city of God, the holy habitation of the Most High (Elyon)', mentioned elsewhere in connection with Jerusalem (cf. Isa. 8.5; 33.21; Ezek. 47.1ff.; Joel 3.18; Zech. 14.8), while in Ps. 48.7 we read of the shattering of ships, apparently within sight of Jerusalem (cf. v. 8), a mythical motif also associated with Jerusalem in Isa. 33.21-23. Miller also appeals to the fact that in the work of the Chronicler the Korahites are not singled out as one of the three groups of Jerusalem temple singers in 1 Chron. 5.31-48, but they appear rather as temple gatekeepers (cf. 1 Chron. 26.1). However, they do appear as singers in the Jerusalem temple in 2 Chron. 20.19, a verse which Miller seeks too readily to dismiss.

Goulder's case for attributing the Korahite psalms originally to a Danite location, a view previously held by J.P. Peters, is also tenuous. (He accepts that they were employed in Jerusalem from the seventh century BC, thus explaining the references to Zion.) 'The heights of the north', as Goulder renders the phrase in Ps. 48.2, is now brought in to support a location at the northerly sanctuary of Dan, while the river of Ps. 46.4 is held to denote the river Jordan. However, for the reasons already given, it seems that the references are rather mythical imagery relating to Jerusalem. Already in the eighth century BC, Isaiah appears to draw on traditions from Psalm 46 and to relate them to Jerusalem (cf. Isa. 7.14; 8.5ff.; 17.12-14). Again, Goulder appeals to Psalm 42, where reference is made to the psalmist's being at Mt Hermon and the land of Jordan (v. 6), which were close to Dan, but the context in the psalm clearly implies that the psalmist is thirsting for God as he is a long way from Yahweh's sanctuary, presumably the Jerusalem temple. It is difficult to see, therefore, how this psalm supports the view that the Korahite psalms were part of the regular Danite liturgy. In conclusion, there seem no convincing reasons for rejecting the view that the Korahite psalms originated in the Jerusalem cult, as the many references to Zion suggest.

The Psalms of Asaph

Psalms 50 and 73–83 are ascribed to Asaph. It seems that Psalm 50 somehow became separated from the rest, so that it now forms a bridge between the first collection of Korahite psalms (Psalms 42–49) and the second collection of Davidic psalms (Psalms 51–57). Asaph appears in Chronicles as a temple musician and singer in the time of David (1 Chron. 15.16-19; 16.4-5, 7, 37) and the sons of Asaph similarly appear in this role in later times (1 Chron. 25.1ff; 2 Chron. 5.12; 20.14; 29.13; 35.15; Ezra 2.41; 3.10; Neh. 7.44; 11.22). The Asaphite psalms seem to derive their origin from the guild of the sons of Asaph. It is strange that the headings ascribe these psalms to Asaph himself rather than the sons of Asaph, since they are manifestly from a later date than David, attesting for example the destruction of the Jerusalem temple in 586 BC (cf. Psalms 74; 79).

These psalms tend to be characterized by certain distinctive features, thus lending credence to the view that they did indeed form a separate collection prior to their inclusion in our Psalter. These features include the following:

(1) They are all concerned in some way or other with divine judgment, whether on Israel (Psalms 50; 77; 78; 80; 81), Jerusalem (Psalms 74; 79), the foreign nations (Psalms 75; 76; 83), wicked individuals (Psalm 73), or the gods (Psalm 82). The subject is, however, treated in quite different ways within these psalms.

(2) A fair number of these psalms appeal to Yahweh's mighty deeds in the past (whether in history or at creation) as a motivation for Yahweh to act in the present or by way of warning or exhortation to the people. Especially prominent are the events of the period of the Exodus (Pss. 77.11-20; 78.11-53; 80.8-11; 81.4-7), though we also read of the settlement and conquest of Canaan (Ps. 78.53-54), events in the period of the Judges (Pss. 78.60-66; 83.9-12), and Yahweh's victory over the powers of chaos and ordering of the world at the time of creation (Ps. 74.12-17).

(3) There is a remarkably high number of allusions to Israel as a flock of sheep, with Yahweh as its shepherd (Pss. 74.1; 77.20; 78.52 [cf. 70–72]; 79.13; 80.1), more so than in the whole of the rest of the Psalter.

(4) Again, there is a surprisingly high number of references to the northern tribes of Israel, especially under the name of Joseph (Pss. 77.15; 78.9, 67; 80.1f.; 81.5). There is only one other reference to Joseph in the whole of the rest of the Psalter (Ps. 105.17), and there it is as an individual rather than as a tribal name.

(5) There is, again, an above average number of divine oracles in these psalms (Pss. 50; 75.2-5; 81.6-16; 82.2-7).

(6) Overwhelmingly these psalms focus on the community as a whole rather than on the individual (Psalm 73 is the one exception). Contrast the so-called Davidic psalms, where individual laments are so preponderant.

Because of the evident concern of a number of these psalms for the northern tribes, it has sometimes been supposed that the guild of the Asaphites originated in the north before coming to Jerusalem. This, however, is far from certain. Psalm 78 is markedly anti-northern and the references to Joseph are no doubt conditioned by the particular connection of the Joseph tribes with the Exodus, which also figures prominently in these psalms. Psalm 80 is unlikely to have been actually composed in the north, as some suppose, since it presupposes that Yahweh is enthroned on the cherubim (v. 1), representations of which existed in the Jerusalem temple. But the possibility of some northern background to the Asaphites cannot be ruled out.

With their emphasis on divine judgment, divine oracles and appeals to Yahweh's acts in the past, we seem to have evidence of the prophetic background of these psalms. It is therefore interesting that the Chronicler speaks of Asaph as a seer (2 Chron. 29.30) and of the sons of Asaph and other temple singers and musicians as prophesying (1 Chron. 25.1-6; cf. 2 Chron. 20.14; 35.15). A.R. Johnson has conjectured that the cult prophets of the pre-exilic period were incorporated into the ranks of the temple musicians and singers in the post-exilic period.

The Psalms of Jeduthun

Psalm 39 is headed 'by Jeduthun' (*lîdûtûn*) and Psalms 62 and 77 'according to Jeduthun' (*yedûtûn*). Comparable to Asaph and Heman, Jeduthun is the name used several times in Chronicles (1 Chron. 9.16; 16.38, 41f.; 25.1, 3, 6; 2 Chron. 5.12; 29.14; 35.15) and once in Nehemiah (Neh. 11.17) for a temple musician and singer who lived in the time of David and Solomon, and whose descendants also functioned in the same way. He seems to be equated with Ethan (1 Chron. 15.17, 19; cf. 1 Kgs 4.31), to whom is attributed Psalm 89 (see below). Mowinckel, however, thinks that Jeduthun in the psalm headings is not a personal name at all but a noun meaning 'confession'. But over against this stands the fact that a reference to the temple musician Jeduthun is fully expected, since other temple musicians known from Chronicles appear too in the headings (Asaph, sons of Korah, etc.). However, the suggestion has also been made that Jeduthun in the psalms is a psalm tone and that this became transformed into a personal name in Chronicles. The reason some have been sceptical that Jeduthun in the psalm headings is the name of the temple musician is the occurrence of the preposition *'al* 'according to' before the word in Psalms 62 and 77, which is somewhat

strange before a personal name, but it may be that we should
understand 'after Jeduthun', i.e. 'after the manner of
Jeduthun's music-making'.

A Psalm of Ethan the Ezrahite

Psalm 89 is ascribed to Ethan the Ezrahite, who also appears
in 1 Kgs 4.31 as a wise man in the time of Solomon. Presumably the editor of the heading of Psalm 89 equated him with
Ethan, the temple musician and singer in the time of David (1
Chron. 15.17, 19), who in turn seems to be equated with
Jeduthun, as was noted above. However, in 1 Chron. 2.6 Ethan,
alongside Heman and the others of 1 Kgs 4.31, appears as the
son of Zerah (cf. 'Ezrahite') and the grandson of Judah and
Tamar, long before the time of David and Solomon.

A Psalm of Heman the Ezrahite

Psalm 88 is ascribed to this person, though the heading also
calls it a psalm of the sons of Korah. Heman the Ezrahite also
appears in 1 Kgs 4.31, alongside Ethan, as a wise man in the
time of Solomon. Presumably the editor of the heading of
Psalm 88 equated him with Heman, the temple musician and
singer in the time of David (1 Chron. 15.17, 19), although in 1
Chron. 2.6 Heman is the son of Zerah and grandson of Judah
and Tamar.

A Psalm of Solomon

Psalms 72 and 127 are attributed to Solomon in their headings,
but this is a late tradition. Psalm 127, in fact, is a post-exilic
psalm, and although Psalm 72 is a pre-exilic royal psalm, it is
unlikely to be by Solomon. However, it is not difficult to see how
these psalms came to be ascribed to this king. The grand
imperial rule depicted in Psalm 72 would have recalled
Solomon, especially the references to the tribute from Sheba in
vv. 10 and 15 (cf. the queen of Sheba in 1 Kgs 10) and possibly
the allusion to the king of Tarshish in v. 10 (cf. 'ships of
Tarshish' in 1 Kgs 10.22) and 'the royal son' in v. 1, which
would rule out David. Psalm 127.1's statement, 'Unless the

Lord builds the house, those who build it labour in vain' was wrongly interpreted as referring to the temple, which Solomon built, and 'his beloved' in v. 2 was possibly also connected with Solomon, who is called Jedidiah ('beloved of the Lord') in 2 Sam. 12.25.

A Prayer of Moses, the Man of God

Just one psalm, Psalm 90, is attributed to Moses, but no critical scholar takes this seriously. The psalm itself gives no indication of having come from such an early period and this is clearly a late attribution.

(On Songs of the Steps [or Ascents], see above, Chapter 4.)

Further Reading

On the ordering of the psalms:

A. Arens, *Die Psalmen im Gottesdienst des alten Bundes* (Trierer theologische Studien, 11), Trier, 1961. (Lectionary approach.)

J. Heinemann, 'The Triennial Lectionary Cycle', *JJS* 19 (1968), 41-48. (Rejects the possibility of a lectionary approach.)

G.H. Wilson, *The Editing of the Hebrew Psalter* (SBL Dissertation Series, 76), Chico: Scholars, 1985.

On David in the Psalm headings, and the Davidic Psalms:

F.F. Bruce, 'The Earliest Old Testament Interpretation', *OTS* 17 (1972), 44-52.

B.S. Childs, 'Psalm Titles and Midrashic Exegesis', *JSS* 16 (1971), 137-50.

M.D. Goulder, *The Prayers of David (Psalms 51–72). Studies in the Psalter, II* (JSOT Supplement Series, 102), Sheffield: JSOT, 1990.

S. Mowinckel, *The Psalms in Israel's Worship* 2, 98-101.

On the Psalms of the sons of Korah:

M.D. Goulder, *The Psalms of the Sons of Korah* (JSOT Supplement Series, 20), Sheffield: JSOT, 1982.

J.M. Miller, 'The Korahites of Southern Judah', *CBQ* 32 (1970), 58-68.

G. Wanke, *Die Zionstheologie der Korachiten* (BZAW, 97), Berlin: Töpelmann, 1966.

On the Psalms of Asaph:

M.J. Buss, 'The Psalms of Asaph and Korah', *JBL* 82 (1963), 382-92.

K.-J. Illman, *Thema und Tradition in den Asaf-Psalmen* (Publications of the Research Institute of the Åbo Akademi Foundation, 12), Åbo: Åbo Akademi Forskningsinstitut, 1976.

H.P. Nasuti, *Tradition History and the Psalms of Asaph* (SBL Dissertation Series, 88), Atlanta: Scholars, 1988.

8

THE THEOLOGY OF THE PSALMS AND THE HISTORY OF THEIR INTERPRETATION BY THE JEWS AND IN THE CHRISTIAN CHURCH

The Theology of the Psalms

Yahweh and the Gods

PSALM. 53.1 (= PS. 14.1) DECLARES, 'The fool says in his heart, "There is no God"'. This is not an expression of theoretical atheism, which probably did not exist in ancient Israel, but rather of practical atheism. Cf. v. 1b, 'They are corrupt, doing abominable iniquity; there is none that does good'.

Similarly, for the most part, it is a practical rather than a theoretical monotheism which is to be found in the Psalter. Israel is to worship only Yahweh—cf. the echo of the beginning of the Decalogue in Ps. 81.9-10, 'There shall be no strange god among you; you shall not bow down to a foreign god. I am the Lord your God, who brought you up out of the land of Egypt.' This is not the same as saying that other gods do not exist. However, the post-exilic passages about the idols of the nations in Pss. 115.4-8 and 135.15-18 clearly do reflect a belief in absolute monotheism. When the existence of other gods is not denied, it is Yahweh's incomparability and superiority which are emphasized, for example Pss. 95.3, 'For the Lord is a great God, and a great king above all gods'; 97.7, '... all gods bow down before him'. In a number of instances in the Psalter the gods are regarded as forming Yahweh's heavenly council, a belief somewhat analogous to that of Canaanite religion where the gods (the sons of El) constituted the court of the supreme god El, as we know from the Ugaritic texts (cf. Pss. 29.1; 82.1, 6; 89.5-7). However, Psalm 82 stands apart in that here the gods are sentenced to death for their maladminis- tration of the nations (cf. vv. 6-7). An interesting way of approaching monotheism!

Yahweh as Creator

Yahweh's creation of the world is a recurrent theme in the psalms. Quite often it is associated with Yahweh's conflict with the chaos waters or dragon, which preceded the effective work of creation. Sometimes this event is appealed to in laments as a reminder of Yahweh's past triumphs (cf. Pss. 74.12-17; 89.9- 13), and here the dragon is referred to, named either as Levia- than or Rahab. More commonly we hear of the sea or waters subdued at creation (cf. Pss. 65.6-7; 93.3-4; 104.5-9); in Ps. 33.6-7 a demythologization has taken place in so far as the conflict with the waters appears to have become simply a job of work, as in Genesis 1. In Ps. 29.3, 10, God's supremacy over the waters is a sign of his effective lordship over the creation. This was the theme associated with Yahweh's kingship at the feast of Tabernacles. One of the passages cited, Ps. 104.5-9, forms part of a larger whole extolling Yahweh's lordship over crea- tion. This psalm also shows evidence of dependence on Pharaoh Akhenaten's hymn to the sun, and in turn seems to be one of the sources underlying Genesis 1, where the order of creation is strikingly similar.

The splendour of the universe was held to declare the glory of God. As Psalm 19 declares, in words made famous by Haydn's splendid composition, 'The heavens are telling the glory of God; and the firmament proclaims his handiwork'. In other places in the psalms the various parts of creation are exhorted to praise Yahweh (Pss. 96.11f.; 98.7f.). It is in the hymns in the Psalter that Yahweh's creation of the world is characteristically alluded to. The creation of mankind is referred to much less frequently in the psalms than the cre- ation of the world. The classic passage is Ps. 8.3-8. (See below under 'humanity'.)

Yahweh's mighty deeds in history

Pride of place here goes to the Exodus, the deliverance of the Hebrew slaves from oppression in Egypt in the time of Moses (cf. Pss. 77.16ff.; 78.11-13, 42-51; 80.8; 81.5, 10; 105.26-36; 106.7-12; 114.1, 3, 5; 135.8-9; 136.10-15), and following on from this the wanderings in the wilderness (cf. Ps. 68.7ff.; 78.14ff.; 81.7; 105.37-41; 106.14-33; 114.4, 6, 8; 136.16), and the settlement of Israel in Canaan (cf. Psalms 78.54-55; 105.44; 114.3, 5; 135.10-12; 136.17-22). A few psalms, such as Pss. 78; 105, and 106 are taken up with these events to a very great extent (see above, Chapter 4, under 'Historical Psalms'). The exile, understood as God's judgment on the nation's sin, provides the setting of a number of psalms, including Psalms 74 and 79, which lament the fall of the temple, and Ps. 137, which alludes to the life of the Jewish exiles 'by the rivers of Babylon'. God's restoration of the Jews from exile provides the setting of Ps. 126 and quite likely Psalm 85 as well. The Jews found it less easy to perceive God at work in history in the post-exilic period, and this is reflected in the absence of such references in the psalms.

Yahweh's Attributes

One image employed of Yahweh in the psalms is that of king (e.g. Pss. 24.7-10; 29.10; 48.2; 74.12; 93.1; 95.3; 96.10; 97.1; 98.6; 99.1). This epithet too was borrowed from the Canaanites. Some passages associate Yahweh's kingship with his victory over the chaos waters (cf. Pss. 29.10; 74.12ff.; 93.1ff.), which clearly derives ultimately from the Canaanite god Baal, whose victory over the god Yam (sea) formed the basis of his kingship, as we know from a myth preserved in the Ugaritic texts (Gibson, 37-45). The Old Testament on a number of occasions connects Yahweh's kingship with his creation of the world (cf. Pss. 74.12ff.; 93.1ff.; 95.3f.; 96.10). The theme of Yahweh's enthronement over the chaos waters at the time of creation was re-enacted at the celebrations at the feast of Tabernacles, as we have seen in Chapter 5. As king, Yahweh was envisaged as enthroned on the cherubim in the Holy of Holies of the

Jerusalem temple (Ps. 80.1), and the gods formed as it were his
heavenly court (Pss. 29.1; 82.1, 6; 89.5-7). It should be noted
that the images of Yahweh as shepherd (cf. Ps. 23.1ff.; 80.1)
and judge (e.g. Pss. 82.1; 96.13) are alternative ways of referring to his kingship.

Another way in which Yahweh's greatness is indicated in
the psalms is by referring to him as the Most High (Heb.
'elyôn, cf. Pss. 46.4; 47.2; 82.6; 87.5; 97.9). However, while it
serves to highlight his supremacy, this term is not merely an
epithet but represents the appropriation to Yahweh of the
name of a West Semitic god, known elsewhere from an Aramaic treaty from Sefire and from Philo of Byblos. In Gen.
14.18-20, 22, God Most High (El-Elyon) is the name of the pre-
Israelite, Jebusite (Canaanite) god of Jerusalem, whose priest
was Melchizedek, and it was doubtless from there that the
Israelites appropriated the name for Yahweh following
David's conquest of the city.

As elsewhere in the Old Testament, Yahweh in the psalms is
presented as a holy God. On a number of occasions he is called
the Holy One of Israel (Pss. 71.22; 78.41; 89.18). This term is
better known from the book of Isaiah, both in the words of the
prophet known as First Isaiah (e.g. Isa. 1.4; 5.19) and in Second
Isaiah (e.g. Isa. 41.14; 49.7), and indeed it has sometimes been
supposed that it was First Isaiah who coined the expression.
However, there are good grounds for believing that he derived
the phrase from the cult traditions of Jerusalem, for it occurs
already in Ps. 78.41, a psalm which, as we have seen, there is
every reason to believe is earlier than Isaiah. Interestingly,
another aspect of Isaiah's presentation of Yahweh's holiness
appears to have its background in Jerusalem cult traditions
attested in the psalms. This concerns Isaiah 6, where in the
midst of the prophet's vision of Yahweh as king he hears the
seraphim cry out 'Holy, holy, holy...' We may compare Psalm
99, where Yahweh's holiness is extolled three times in the
course of a psalm celebrating his kingship (vv. 3, 5, 9; cf. v. 1).

One term which is used remarkably frequently of Yahweh
in the psalms is the Hebrew word *ḥesed* Altogether it occurs
there over one hundred times. It is variously translated as
steadfast love, mercy, loyalty or lovingkindness, etc., and
denotes Yahweh's characteristic attitude towards the Israel-

ites, both collectively and individually. Psalmists repeatedly 25.6; 31.16) and it is constantly given as a reason for praising him (cf. Psalms 117; 136).

Because of his lovingkindness, Yahweh is a God who delivers his people, both individually and collectively. Sometimes the verb 'save' (Heb. *yāša'*) is used, and it is particularly frequent in the imperative form in lament psalms in appeals to the deity (e.g. Pss. 7.1; 22.21; 28.9). Sometimes the verb 'redeem' is used in connection with God, whether the Hebrew root used be *pādââh* or *g ā'al*. Whereas the former root (attested for example in Pss. 25.22; 26.11; 71.23; 78.42) had a background in business transactions, the latter (cf. Pss. 74.2; 106.10; 107.2; 119.154) was specific to family law, where the *gō'ēl* ('redeemer') was a kinsman who redeemed a relative from slavery (Lev. 25.47-55), bought back their lost land (Lev. 25.23-34) or undertook marriage to a female relative so as to remove her widowhood (Ruth 4). As employed of God, therefore, the term had warm personal overtones.

Various terms are used to give expression to the psalmist's confidence in Yahweh. For example, God is spoken of as a rock (Heb. *sela'* or *ṣûr*, e.g. Pss. 18.2; 31.2-3), or fortress (e.g. Pss. 94.22; 14.42) and as one under whose wings one shelters (e.g. Pss. 17.8; 63.7). Attempts have sometimes been made to connect the rock and wings with cultic realities in the temple, so that the rock has been related to the sacred rock in the Holy of Holies (currently the centrepiece of the Muslim mosque called The Dome of the Rock in Jerusalem) and the wings have been equated with those of the cherubim, the winged sphinxes in the Holy of Holies (above the Ark) which constituted Yahweh's throne. However, there are problems with both these views. There is no real evidence that the sacred rock in Jerusalem was in the Holy of Holies, and indeed, if it was, further problems would arise in our understanding of the temple's location which will not be discussed here. With regard to references to the psalmist's sheltering under Yahweh's wings, it seems more likely that Yahweh is here being portrayed as a protective (mother) bird, since not only is this image used elsewhere of Yahweh in Deut. 32.11, but the wings are specifically said to be his in the psalms.

Yahweh's Presence

The Hebrews conceived of Yahweh as both transcendent and immanent, and this is reflected in the Psalter. He is regarded as dwelling at once in heaven and in the temple on Mt Zion. Cf. Ps. 11.4, 'The Lord is in his holy temple, the Lord's throne is in heaven...'

Yahweh's presence was associated with Mt Zion from the time of David, when he brought up the sacred Ark into Jerusalem (2 Sam. 6), and with the temple in Jerusalem from the time of Solomon, when the Ark was taken up into that sanctuary. As we have noted earlier, Psalm 132 indicates a repeated cultic bringing up of the Ark into the sanctuary at the feast of Tabernacles (cf. Pss. 24.7-10; 47.5; 68.1, 18). In addition to these probable references to the Ark there are doubtless others. Sometimes it appears to be spoken of as Yahweh's power ('ōz) or glory *(kābôd* or *tip'eret)*. This is clearly the case in Ps. 78.61 (cf. 1 Sam. 4.21f.), and may well be the case also in Pss. 63.2 and 96.6 (cf. also Ps. 132.8). Although the Ark was associated with Yahweh's presence, it was not his throne, contrary to what some earlier scholars have thought. It was the cherubim (winged sphinxes) above the Ark in the Holy of Holies which represented Yahweh's earthly throne (cf. 1 Sam. 4.4; 2 Sam. 6.2; Pss. 80.1; 99.1), so that the Ark functioned rather as a footstool (cf. 1 Chron. 28.2; Pss. 132.7; and probably 99.5). Yahweh's presence in the temple was thought of as guaranteeing the security of Zion. Nations may besiege it but it will remain inviolable. We find this motif in Psalms 46; 48; and 76. Isaiah later qualified this tradition by emphasizing the need for faith (cf. Isa. 7.9), if God was to defend Zion.

It has sometimes been claimed, especially by H.J. Franken, that the Psalter attests experience of God's presence in a mystical sense. If by mysticism we mean absorption into the deity, this is certainly not the case. If, on the other hand, we mean intimate fellowship and communion with God, then one may speak of mysticism in the Psalter. It should be noted, however, that the Psalter suggests that God's presence was particularly apprehended in the course of worship in the temple (cf. Pss. 23.5-6; 27.4; 42.1-2; 84.1-7, 10). We should remember that

Isaiah's majestic vision of God in Isaiah 6, which contains echoes of Psalm 99, was experienced in the temple.

At the same time, as Psalm 139 eloquently declares, it is impossible to escape from God's presence: 'Whither shall I go from thy spirit? Or whither shall I flee from thy presence? If I ascend to heaven, thou art there! If I make my bed in Sheol, thou art there!' (vv. 7-8).

Humanity

The classic passage in the psalms on the dignity and role of humanity is to be found in Ps. 8.3-8, which bears comparison with Gen. 1.26ff. By way of contrast, the transitoriness of human life is indicated in the psalms by the image of the withering of grass or the flower of the field (Pss. 90.5f.; 102.11; 103.15f.; cf. Isa. 40.6f.; Job 14.1f.) and by the comparison of humanity with breath (Pss. 39.5; 62.9) or a shadow (Ps. 102.11). The overtones of weakness can also be conveyed by the use of the word 'flesh' (Heb. *bāśār*, Ps. 56.4; 78.39).

For the Hebrews the human person was not an incarnated soul but an animated body. The spirit (*rûaḥ*) which humans possessed was God's own Spirit, which was returned at death (Ps. 104.29f.). Although the word *nepeš* is frequently translated 'soul' in the English Bible, we need to remember that this is not 'soul' in a Platonic dualistic sense. Rather it denotes the total person (cf. Gen. 2.7, where breath of life + dust of the earth = living soul). As such it can sometimes be translated 'life', e.g. Ps. 30.3, 'O Lord, thou hast brought up my life from Sheol' (cf. Ps. 16.10); or by the first person pronoun, e.g. Ps. 26.9, 'Sweep *me* not away with sinners'. Since the *nepeš* was the place of the feelings, the rendering 'soul' can also be appropriate, e.g. Ps. 42.6, 'My soul is cast down within me'. It can even mean 'desire', as in Ps. 35.25, 'Let them not say to themselves, "Aha, we have our heart's desire!"'. *Nepeš* can also mean throat or neck, e.g. Ps. 69.1, 'Save me, O God! For the waters have come up to my neck', and this physical sense seems to have been its original meaning (cf. Akkadian *napištu*, Ugaritic *npš*).

The human personality also came to be denoted by terms denoting other parts of the human body. Thus, the kidneys

(Heb. *kelāyôt*) are used in this sense in Pss. 7.9; 16.7; 26.2; 73.21 (translated 'heart(s)' in the RSV); and the word 'heart' (Heb. *lēb* or *lēbāb*) is used frequently with various connotations, whether as the seat of feelings (Pss. 25.17; 27.14; 119.32), desire (Ps. 21.2) or reason. Finally, it is probable that the liver is also used to denote the human personality in Pss. 7.5; 16.9; 30.12; 57.8; 108.1. In all these cases the Hebrew text actually speaks of the psalmist's 'glory' (Heb. *kābôd)*, but most scholars emend to *kābêd* 'liver'. Although some scholars (e.g. J.W. McKay) have attempted to defend 'glory' as original, so that it would allude to human dignity, deriving from God, this does seem a rather strange term to use for the human personality. In favour of the simple emendation to *kābēd* 'liver' stands the fact that the liver is used in this sense elsewhere in the Old Testament in Lam. 2.11 as well as in other Semitic languages (Akkadian, Ugaritic and Arabic). Its use is thus of a piece with that of other parts of the body used in Hebrew in a psychological sense (bowels, kidneys, heart).

Sheol (the Underworld) and Life after Death

For the Hebrews the earth was thought of as a flat, circular disk, and above it was the firmament, a blue solid structure arching the earth, and supported by the pillars of heaven. Rain came through the 'windows of heaven' in the firmament, above which were the cosmic waters, which existed also *below* the earth, and were connected with the earth's springs, seas and rivers. The earth was supported by pillars. Underneath the earth was also the realm of the dead, the name for which in Hebrew is Sheol (etymology uncertain but probably meaning 'devastation' from the verb *šā'â* 'to be devastated' + afformative *l)*. In conception Sheol is very similar to the Greek Hades, by which it is rendered in the Greek Septuagint translation. It was a gloomy, subterranean cavern to which all the dead went without distinction, where they endured a shadowy existence. It was dark (Pss. 88.6; 143.3) and silent (Ps. 115.17), and is often referred to as the Pit (Heb. *bôr* in Pss. 28.1; 30.3; 40.2; 88.4, 6; 143.7; *šaḥat* in Pss. 30.9; 55.23; *be'ēr* in Ps. 69.15) and sometimes as 'the depths' or 'the depths of the earth' (various Hebrew terms are used: Pss. 63.9; 71.20; 86.13; 130.1).

Sometimes Sheol is depicted as lying immediately below the surface of the earth (cf. Num. 16.31ff.), but elsewhere it is thought of as lying beneath the subterranean waters (cf. Ps. 18.4f. = 2 Sam. 22.5f.; Jon. 2.22ff.). The latter concept accounts for the references to the mire or miry bog in connection with Sheol in Ps. 40.2; 69.2, 14, and also explains the allusions to feet slipping in Pss. 66.9; 94.18. Sheol was a realm from which there was no return (Ps. 88.8; Job 7.9-10; 10.21); we may compare its Akkadian description as the 'land of no return' *(erşet lā tāri).* Moreover, Sheol was thought of as a region cut off from Yahweh (cf. Pss. 6.5; 88.10-12). Psalm 88 is particularly noteworthy for the gloomy picture of Sheol which it depicts. We do, however, find a certain development in Psalm 139, where we find the belief that no region of the universe, even Sheol, is outside Yahweh's presence: 'If I ascend to heaven, thou art there! If I make my bed in Sheol, thou art there!'

Obviously, to fall into the sphere of the underworld was a terrible fate for the Hebrew. The psalms are therefore full of allusions to the desire for rescue from Sheol and thanksgivings which are given for deliverance from death. However, we need to remember, as A.R. Johnson emphasized, that what for us would be a weak form of life (illness, various kinds of distress) could be spoken of by the Israelites as a form of death.

However, there are two passages which may well reflect an emerging belief in a worthwhile afterlife. Both may be wisdom psalms (the former certainly so) and both reflect on the prosperity of the wicked and the suffering of the righteous. Ps. 49.14-15 concludes, 'Like sheep they (*sc.* the wicked) are appointed for Sheol; Death shall be their shepherd; straight to the grave they descend, and their form shall waste away. But God will ransom my soul from the power of Sheol, for he will receive me.' There are those, e.g. A.F. Kirkpatrick, who have thought that this refers to a temporary reprieve from death for the righteous. However, it is perhaps more probable that this does refer to life after death, since otherwise the righteous would be worse off, not better off, than the wicked, sharing with them the fate of death, but also experiencing ill fortune in the present.

Another possible example occurs in Psalm 73. In v. 23 the psalmist consoles himself with the thought of his present communion with God: 'Nevertheless I am continually with thee; thou dost hold my right hand'. Then he goes on (v. 24): 'Thou dost guide me with thy counsel, and afterward thou wilt receive me to glory'. The crucial question, of course, is what is meant by 'afterward'. Again, there are those who think it refers to the period after the psalmist's present distress. However, since he already has communion with Yahweh (v. 23), it seems more natural to suppose that 'afterward' refers to the time after death. In any case, 'afterward thou wilt receive me to glory' seems an odd way of alluding to the resumption of normal living in this life.

Some scholars have also seen references to life after death in Ps. 16.10-11, but this is less likely. Even more unlikely are the views of M.J. Dahood, whose unusual commentary on the psalms has already been referred to. Dahood finds a much more robust belief in immortality in the Psalter than has generally been supposed, but his interpretations are highly dubious and have failed to convince many scholars.

Universalism

For the psalms, as for the rest of the Old Testament, Yahweh is not only the God of Israel but the God of the whole world, a belief that follows naturally from the fact that he was regarded as the creator of the world and eventually became conceived of not only as the supreme but also as the only God. Accordingly, in the psalms we find invitations to the nations to praise God (e.g. Pss. 47.1; 66.1-4, 8; 67.3-7; 68.32; 100.1-2) as well as allusions to the future conversion/submission of the gentiles to Yahweh (cf. Pss. 22.27-28; 47.9; 65.2; 68.29, 31; 86.9; 87.4-6; 102.15, 22).

The King

As we have seen in Chapter 6, the king—by which is meant the Davidic ruler in Jerusalem—is portrayed in the psalms as standing in a special relationship to Yahweh. He is God's vicegerent, and as such he is Yahweh's anointed one (Ps. 132.10, 17), son of God by adoption (Ps. 2.7), and a priest for ever after the order of Melchizedek (Ps. 110.4). His vocation is to rule over the world in justice and righteousness (Psalm 72), to obey Yahweh's commandments (Psalm 101), and to do battle against his enemies in God's strength (Pss. 18; 20; 21). The Davidic king lived in a covenant relationship with Yahweh, whereby his dynasty would abide for ever, provided he was obedient (Ps. 89.3-4, 19-37); however, Ps. 89.38-51 appear to reflect the ending of the Davidic monarchy and Yahweh's apparent rejection of this covenant. In the post-exilic period, when there was no longer an Israelite king on the throne, the royal psalms were interpreted in an eschatological sense as referring to an ideal future ruler—whom we should call the Messiah—though the Old Testament itself employs this term only of the current king.

Sacrifice

There are many references to sacrifice in the psalms, and as we have seen earlier, together with other cultic allusions, these are an indication of the Psalter's liturgical origin. The two main types of sacrifice were the peace offerings (Heb. *šᵉlāmîm*, singular *šelem*), referred to simply as sacrifices (*zᵉbāḥîm*, singular *zebaḥ*) in the Psalter (cf. Pss. 4.5; 27.6; 54.6; 116.17), and burnt offerings (*'ōlôt*, singular *'ōlâ*), alluded to in Pss. 20.3; 66.13, 25. In the case of the peace offering, the animal was eaten by the worshippers and the priests, with the exception of the fat, which was burnt. The underlying idea seems to have been that of communion. On the other hand, the burnt offerings, as their name implies, were wholly consumed on the altar, apart from the hide. The underlying idea seems to have been that of a gift. The Psalter also mentions the thank-offering (*tōdâ*, Pss. 56.12; 100 (superscription); 107.22; 116.17), vows (*nᵉdārîm*, Pss. 22.25; 50.14; 56.12; 61.5, 8; 65.1; 66.13; 76.11; 116.14), and the freewill offering (*nᵉdābâ*, Ps. 54.6), all of which were forms of peace offering. We also read of the offering (*minḥâ*, Pss. 20.3; 86.8). Originally this term denoted sacrifices of any kind, whether grain or animal, but in the post-exilic period it was restricted to cereal offerings and oil.

The Psalter does not offer any proper theological explanation of the meaning of sacrifice, any more than do other parts of the Old Testament. However, it does contain some interesting 'anti-sacrificial' passages, Pss. 40.6; 50.8-15; 51.16f. (cf. vv. 18.5), to which may be added Pss. 69.30f. and 141.2. Anti-sacrificial passages are also found elsewhere in the Old Testament, especially in the prophets (cf. 1 Sam. 15.22; Isa. 1.11ff.; Jer. 6.20; 7.21f.; Hos. 6.6; Amos 5.21ff.; Mic. 6.6ff.; Prov. 21.3). There used to be a tendency to find in these passages evidence of opposition to sacrifice *per se*, but in general scholars have come to reject this. For the most part what we seem to have is an affirmation that ethical righteousness and obedience to God are more important than sacrifices. Thus, with regard to Ps. 40.6, the words 'Sacrifice and offering thou dost not require' are followed by the declaration 'but thou hast dug ears for me', which seems to be a curious way of saying 'but thou hast given me an open ear', i.e. Yahweh demands hearing and obedience (cf. Ps. 69.30f.). Ps. 50.8-15, likewise, does not seem to be criticizing sacrifice *per se*, since v. 3 actually states 'I do not reprove you for your sacrifices. . . ' What appears to be opposed here is the notion that Yahweh is dependent on sacrifices for food and drink—cf. vv. 12-13, 'If I were hungry, I would not tell you; for the world and all that is in it are mine. Do I eat the flesh of bulls, or drink the blood of goats?'

The moving penitential psalm Psalm 51, the *Miserere*, contains in vv. 16-17 the striking words, 'For thou hast no delight in sacrifices; were I to give a burnt offering, thou wouldst not be pleased. The sacrifice acceptable to God is a broken spirit; a broken and contrite heart, O God, thou wilt not despise.' The psalmist presumably rejects sacrifice here because it is inappropriate in his particular case; he has committed a grievous sin (e.g. murder or adultery), for which the Law provided no sacrifice as a means of atonement, so all he could do was to throw himself on Yahweh's mercy in abject surrender and humility. Verses 18-19 are surely the work of a later glossator, dating from the exile or early post-exilic period, whose mundane statement that right sacrifices will be offered when the walls of Jerusalem have been rebuilt appears to miss the profound point that the psalm is making. It illustrates the disadvantage in believing, as B.S. Childs appears to do, that it is always preferable to read the Old Testament text theologically in its final, canonical form! Finally, it may be noted that a spiritualization of a cult concept in some ways comparable to Ps.

51.17 may be found in Ps. 141.2, 'Let my prayer be counted as incense before thee, and the lifting up of my hands as an evening sacrifice!'

Ethics and the Law

The Psalter is the embodiment of cultic worship, and it is clear that ethics were important in this context. Psalms 15 and 24 both embody entrance liturgies, setting out the requirements of those who would enter the temple, and in both cases we find that it is ethical, not ritual demands that are made.

There are echoes of the Decalogue in both Psalms 50 and 81, though the latter alludes only to the introduction and first commandment (vv. 9-10). Psalm 50, which seems to reflect a cultic re-enactment of the Sinai pericope in Exodus 19 (cf. v. 3); 20 (cf. vv. 16ff.); and 24 (cf. v. 5), echoes a number of the ethical stipulations of the Decalogue in vv. 16ff. (theft, adultery and false witness). Psalms 50 and 81 suggest that the Decalogue may have been recited at some stage in a covenant renewal festival.

The high ethical standard required of the ordinary Israelite was also expected of the king, as Psalms 72 and 101 make clear (cf. Deut. 17.14-20). Throughout the Psalter there is a strong sense of opposition of the righteous and the wicked, in which a strong ethical emphasis is involved. The Law (Torah), which became increasingly dominant in post-exilic Judaism, is especially the subject of Psalms 1; 19B; and 119.

One feature of the psalms which tends to disturb the modern sensitive reader is the imprecatory element. Curses against enemies abound, sometimes in contexts which appear otherwise sublime, such as Psalm 139. As examples of the most bitter imprecations we may note Pss. 58.6-11; 69.22-28; 83.9-18; 109.6-20; 137.7-9; 149.5-9. The Christian tends to feel that the spirit reflected here falls below Jesus' moral standard of loving one's enemies (Mt. 5.43-8; Lk. 6.27-31). Even John Wesley in the eighteenth century forbade his followers to sing the imprecatory parts of the Psalter. There is no point in trying to explain them away. However, without excusing them, we need to understand the experience of intense suffering that doubtless underlies them, e.g. the experience of exile in an alien land that lies behind Psalm 137. We should also bear in mind the fact that for most of the psalmists there was no meaningful afterlife, so vindication of the righteous, and with it judgment of the wicked, had to take place in this world, and the psalmists were understandably impatient for it. The imprecations may be seen as the obverse of the psalmists' passion for justice.

The most extended curse takes place in Ps. 109.6-19. Occasionally scholars have attempted to argue that these verses represent the curses heaped on the psalmist by his enemies rather than *vice versa*. However, apart from the fact that there is a further imprecation in v. 29, which this interpretation fails to explain, this view comes up against the problem of v. 20a, which, following the extended imprecation of vv. 6-19, most naturally reads, 'May this be the reward of my accusers from the Lord'. The attempt to render 'reward' as 'work' and eliminate 'from the Lord' from the text is entirely forced and arbitrary.

The History of Interpretation of the Psalms by the Jews and in the Christian Church

Jewish Interpretation of the Psalms

The earliest Jewish interpretation is already found in some of the psalm headings that we have studied in the previous chapter. This included the increasing tendency to ascribe psalms to King David, a tendency which continued throughout the intertestamental period. Among the Dead Sea scrolls from Qumran, four (or three) additional apocryphal psalms are attributed to David (Psalms 151 A + B; 154; 155), Psalm 151 already being known from the Septuagint. All of them are also attested in Syriac, but the latter two are not there attributed to David. Some of the fragmentary psalm manuscripts from Qumran attest some of the psalms in an aberrant order from the Hebrew masoretic text (the largest of these is 11QPsª), and it is disputed whether this is simply a liturgical selection (P.W. Skehan) or evidence of fluidity in the ordering of the psalms (especially the last third) at Qumran as late as the first century AD (J.A. Sanders). From Qumran we also have manuscripts commenting on Psalms 37 and 45 (4Q171) and

Psalm 127 (4Q173), as well as one including interpretations of
Psalms 1 and 2 in addition to other biblical passages (4Q
Florilegium or 4Q174), in which the psalms are explained as
referring to events within the Qumran community (cf. the
interpretation of the Old Testament in the New).

The Midrash on the Psalms *(Midrash Tehillim)* is a rather
later work, having grown up by a process of accretion over a
thousand years from the third to the thirteenth centuries AD.
As would be expected from a rabbinical midrash, its interpretation of the text is non-literal in character and is homiletical
rather than strictly exegetical; and the discussion of topics
hardly proceeds in a logical manner. All the psalms are commented on except Psalms 123 and 131, and the commentaries
on Psalms 119–150 are generally agreed to be later than the
previous ones. Although the non-literal, midrashic mode of
exegesis persisted throughout the Middle Ages and beyond,
there were noted Jewish scholars in the medieval period such
as Kimhi who pursued literal exegesis.

Surprisingly, in view of the importance to the rabbis of the
exposition of the psalms, they played little part in the Jewish
liturgy during the talmudic period; in fact, only Psalms 113–
118 (the so-called Egyptian *Hallel*) were employed in that
way. Subsequently, however, partly in response to popular
demand, the psalms gradually penetrated the liturgy and
came to have an important role there, as they still have today.

The Psalms in the New Testament

About one-third of the Old Testament quotations in the New
Testament are from the psalms, a fact which highlights the
importance of the Psalter for primitive Christianity. Although
there are citations from many psalms, Psalms 2, 22, 69, 110,
and 118 are particularly important.

Ps. 2.7 reads, 'You are my son, today I have begotten you'.
Words originally spoken to the king at his coronation are
applied messianically to Christ. They are related to Jesus' bap-
tism (Mt. 3.17; Lk. 3.22), transfiguration (Mt. 17.5; Lk. 9.35),
resurrection (Acts 13.33), and exaltation/ascension (Heb. 1.5;
5.5).

Two verses from another coronation psalm, Psalm 110, are applied a number of times to Christ in the New Testament. Verse 4, 'You are a priest for ever after the order of Melchizedek', is cited several times in the Epistle to the Hebrews (5.6, 10; 6.20; 7.3, 11, 15, 17, 21, 24, 28) to prove the superiority of Jesus' priesthood over that of the Jewish Levitical priesthood. The words about the king's sitting at God's right hand are also echoed a number of times in the New Testament (e.g. Mk 14.62; Acts 2.34f.; Heb. 10.12f.). In Mk 12.35-37 (= Mt. 22.41-46; Lk. 20.41-44) this verse forms the centre of discussion. The question posed here is, if Christ is David's son, how can he also be David's lord? The implied answer is that he is David's greater son.

Psalm 22, an individual lament, is echoed primarily in the gospel passion narratives. Jesus' cry from the cross, *Eloi, Eloi, lama sabachthani*, 'My God, my God, why hast thou forsaken me?', cites Ps. 22.1 in Aramaic: it may well be that these words, which have often been found puzzling, have the wider context of the psalm in mind, which ends on a note of vindication and of the universal coming of the kingdom of God (Ps. 22.22-31). Other echoes of this psalm are the deriding of Jesus and the wagging of heads at him (Mk 15.29; Mt. 27.39; Lk. 23.35; cf. Ps. 22.7), the division of Jesus' garments and casting lots for them (Mk 15.24; Mt. 27.35; Lk. 23.34; Jn 19.24; cf. Ps. 22.18) and the demand that God deliver him (Mt. 27.43; cf. Ps. 22.8). One can obviously debate how far these allusions reflect historical episodes and how far they simply represent the reading of these psalm passages into the passion narrative.

Psalm 69 is another individual lament which is reflected in the passion narrative, at Mk 15.36; Mt. 27.34; Lk. 23.36; Jn 19.29, where Jesus on the cross is offered vinegar. Although the casual reader might take this to be an act of kindness to Jesus, the context in the psalm makes it clear that this is not the case (cf. also Lk. 23.36).

We read in Ps. 118.22f., 'The stone which the builders rejected has become the head of the corner. This is the Lord's doing; it is marvellous in our eyes.' These words are cited a number of times to refer to Jesus' rejection and vindication (Mk 12.10-11; Mt. 21.42; Lk. 20.17; Acts 4.11f.; 1 Pet. 2.7). We know from Jewish sources that this psalm was interpreted messianically. The messianic overtones are clear in the citation from Ps. 118.25f. at the time of Jesus' triumphal entry into Jerusalem on an ass (Mk 11.9f.; Mt. 21.9, 25; Lk. 19.38; Jn 12.13).

There are many other psalms to which the New Testament alludes, but it is not possible to deal with them here.

The Psalms in the Later Christian Church

In the post-New Testament Church the psalms continued to play an important role. Some impression of their pervasive influence may be found in an old book by R.E. Prothero entitled *The Psalms in Human Life*, which is remarkable for the vast number of examples which it cites. All that can be done here is to discuss briefly a few of the commentaries on the psalms by some of the Church's leading figures, and to note their use in liturgy and their important influence on hymn writing.

One of the most famous works by one of the early Church Fathers on the Psalter was Augustine of Hippo's *Enarrationes in Psalmos* (= Expositions on the Psalms). Like much patristic biblical interpretation inspired by the Alexandrian allegorical method, it is worthless as exegesis of the biblical text and its value is restricted to edification. As an example of Augustine's allegorical interpretations of the Psalter we may cite the following regarding Ps. 137.1. '*Rivers of Babylon*. The rivers of Babylon are all things that are here loved, and pass away. Someone, for example, has taken a liking for agriculture, thinking thereby to grow rich, to find occupation for his mind and pleasure. Let him look to the end of it, and see that what he has loved is not a foundation of Jerusalem, but a river of Babylon.'

The school of Antioch—in contrast to that of Alexandria—practised a more literal approach to biblical exegesis. The most critically-minded member of this school was Theodore of Mopsuestia, who accepted only four psalms as messianic: Psalms 2; 8; 44; and 109. In the medieval period the psalms (along with the Pauline epistles) were particularly rich in commentaries, but it was the allegorical approach which prevailed. There were, however, notable exceptions such as

Nicholas of Lyra (d. 1340), who was influenced by medieval Jewish commentators.

Luther wrote more on the psalms even than any New Testament book. His first lectures on the psalms (1513–15) were still wedded to the medieval allegorical mode of interpretation, but his second lectures on the psalms and his exposition of the so-called seven penitential psalms (Psalms 6; 32; 38; 51; 102; 130; 143) reflect the reformers' emphasis on the literal sense of scripture. Luther declared that 'Origen's allegories are not worth so much dirt', though he maintained that one could still use allegories 'as mere spangles and pretty ornaments', like St Paul. Luther's emphasis on the literal meaning of scripture and attention to the Hebrew original rather than simple reliance on the Latin Vulgate marked a great advance on patristic and medieval Christian exegesis. However, he lacked the critical sense of Calvin in that he tended to see the messianic psalms as direct predictions of Christ without any relationship to the king in ancient Israel. The modern critical reader will also be struck by the way in which Luther saw his own times directly addressed in scripture. For example, in his Wartburg interpretation of Psalm 37, he said, 'No one should doubt that our opponents are the ones who are scolded in this psalm, and that we are the ones who are consoled therein'. Psalm 46 was the inspiration for his famous reformation hymn, 'Ein feste Burg ist unser Gott', which was translated into English as 'A safe stronghold our God is still' by Thomas Carlyle.

The other great reformer, John Calvin, wrote a large commentary on the psalms which managed to combine exegetical and philological remarks with practical exposition. In general his exegesis is more scientific than Luther's. With regard to the so-called messianic psalms, Calvin was conscious that they had an original historical meaning in ancient Israel relating to the Israelite king, in addition to their messianic interpretation, which comes in secondarily by way of foreshadowing or typology. His genuine critical interest in the historical setting of the psalms led him to suggest dates for various psalms: e.g. he supposed that Psalm 46 came from the time of the deliverance of Jerusalem from Sennacherib's siege (701 BC).

In the Reformed and Presbyterian Churches arising from the Calvinist and Zwinglian (though not Lutheran or Anglican) Reformation, metrical versions of the psalms have been used in worship. Indeed, originally for these churches the Psalter was the only manual of praise, for other hymns were rejected.

In the Church of England, however, the version of the psalms still widely employed today and found in the Prayer Book represents the sixteenth-century translation of Miles Coverdale. Coverdale's translation of the Psalms had been taken up into the Great Bible, the authorized English Bible at the time of the First and Second Prayer Books of Edward VI (1549 and 1552). When the 1662 revision of the Prayer Book was brought out, Coverdale's version was retained because of its familiarity, although other scriptural passages were taken from the 1611 Authorized (King James) Version of the Bible. Even today, in spite of new translations of the Bible, including new versions of the Psalter that have been specifically prepared for use in worship because of the inaccuracies and archaisms of Coverdale's version (cf. the *Revised Psalter*, a revision of Coverdale in 1963, and *The Psalms. A new translation for worship*, a completely new translation in 1977), his version is still in frequent use.

One way in which the psalms have continued to influence the Church is through the large number of hymns which they have inspired. Some well-known examples include 'O worship the King all glorious above' by Sir Robert Grant, based on W. Kethe (Psalm 104), 'Jesus shall reign where'er the sun' by Isaac Watts (Psalm 72), 'The King of love my shepherd is' by Sir H.W. Baker (Psalm 23), 'Let us with a gladsome mind' by John Milton (Psalm 136), and 'All people that on earth do dwell', in origin a metrical psalm (the Old 100th) by W. Kethe in John Day's Psalter (1561). It is noteworthy that the lament psalms have not been as influential on Christian hymnody as the psalms of praise, though some rare examples include Psalm 130, which has inspired several hymns, including 'Out of the depths I cry to thee' by Martin Luther (translated by Catherine Winkworth), and Psalm 42, which gave rise to N. Tate and N. Brady's well-known hymn 'As pants the hart for cooling streams'.

Further Reading

On the theology of the Psalter generally:

H.-J. Kraus, *Theology of the Psalms*, Minneapolis: Augsburg Publishing House/SPCK, 1986. (The standard work).

H. Ringgren, *The Faith of the Psalmists*, London: SCM, 1963.

L.J. Sabourin, *The Psalms: Their Origin and Meaning*, 1, 65-168.

H. Spieckermann, *Heilsgegenwart: eine Theologie der Psalmen* (FRLANT, 148), Göttingen: Vandenhoeck & Ruprecht, 1989.

On specific theological themes:

R. Albertz, *Weltschöpfung und Menschenschöpfung.*

A.A. Anderson, 'Psalms', in D.A. Carson and H.G.M. Williamson (eds.), *It is Written: Scripture Citing Scripture. Essays in Honour of Barnabas Lindars*, Cambridge: Cambridge University Press, 1988, 56-66.

R.E. Clements, *God and Temple*, Oxford: Blackwell, 1965, ch. 5.

G.H. Davies, 'The Ark in the Psalms', in F.F. Bruce (ed.), *Promise and Fulfilment. Essays Presented to Professor S.H. Hooke*, Edinburgh: T. & T. Clark, 1963, 51-61.

J. Day, *God's Conflict with the Dragon and the Sea.*

D. Eichhorn, *Gott als Fels, Burg und Zuflucht*, Bern and Frankfurt: H. & P. Lang, 1972.

H.J. Franken, *The Mystical Communion with JHWH in the Book of Psalms*, Leiden: Brill, 1954.

J. Gray, *The Biblical Doctrine of the Reign of God*, chs. 2-3.

E. Haglund, *Historical Motifs in the Psalms.*

A.R. Johnson, *The Vitality of the Individual in the Thought of Ancient Israel*, Cardiff: University of Wales Press, 1964.

A.R. Johnson, *The Cultic Prophet and Israel's Psalmody*, Cardiff: University of Wales Press, 1979.

J.W. McKay, '"My Glory"—A Mantle of Praise', *Scottish Journal of Theology* 31 (1978), 167-72.

T.N.D. Mettinger, *In Search of God: The Meaning and Message of the Everlasting Names*, Philadelphia: Fortress, 1987.

H.W. Wolff, *Anthropology of the Old Testament*, London: SCM, 1974.

On the Psalms and their interpretation at Qumran:

G.J. Brooke, *Exegesis at Qumran: 4Q Florilegium in its Jewish Context* (JSOT Supplement Series, 29), Sheffield: JSOT, 1985.

J.A. Sanders, *The Dead Sea Psalms Scroll*, Ithaca: Cornell University Press, 1967.

P.W. Skehan, 'Qumran and Old Testament Criticism', in M. Delcor (ed.), *Qumrân: sa piété, sa théologie et son milieu* (Bibliotheca Ephemeridum theologicarum Lovaniensium, 46), Paris-Gembloux Duculot and Leuven: Leuven University Press, 1978, 163-82.

G. Vermes, *The Dead Sea Scrolls in English*, 3rd edn, London: Penguin Books, 1987, 208-14, 290-92, 293-94 (cf. 165-207).

G.H. Wilson, *The Editing of the Hebrew Psalter*, 63-138.

The Psalms in subsequent Jewish interpretation and life:

J. Baker and E.W. Nicholson, *The Commentary of Rabbi David Kimḥi on Psalms CXX–CL*, Cambridge: Cambridge University Press, 1973.

W.G. Braude, *The Midrash on Psalms*, 2 vols., New Haven: Yale University Press, 1959.

L.I. Rabinowitz, G.E. Silverman and others, 'Psalms, Book of', in *Encyclopaedia Judaica* 13, Jerusalem: Keter, 1971, 1322-34.

On the interpretation of the Psalms in the New Testament:

C.H. Dodd, *According to the Scriptures*, London: Collins, 1952.

D.M. Hay, *Glory at the Right Hand: Psalm 110 in Early Christianity* (SBL Monograph Series, 18), Nashville: Abingdon, 1973.

H.-J. Kraus, *Theology of the Psalms*, 177-203.

B. Lindars, *New Testament Apologetic*, London: SCM, 1961.

On the Psalms in the subsequent Christian Church:

Augustine, *Expositions on the Book of Psalms* (Library of the Fathers), 6 vols., Oxford: Parker, 1847-57.

J. Calvin, *Commentary on the Book of Psalms*, 5 vols. (ed. J. Anderson), Edinburgh: Calvin Translation Society, 1845–49.

J.C. Howell, 'Jerome's Homilies on the Psalter in Bethlehem', in K.G. Hoglund, E.F. Huwiler, J.T. Glass, R.W. Lee (eds.), *The Listening Heart: Essays in Wisdom and the Psalms in Honor of Roland E. Murphy, O. Carm.* (JSOT Supplement Series, 58), Sheffield: JSOT, 1987, 181-97.

L. Jacquet, *Les Psaumes et le coeur de l'homme*.

M. Luther, *Luther's Works*, 10–11 (ed. H.C. Oswalt) and 12–14 (ed. J. Pelikan), St Louis: Concordia Publishing House, 1974–76 and 1955–58.

J.M. Neale and R.F. Littledale, *A Commentary on the Psalms from Primitive and Medieval Writers*, 4 vols., London: Masters, 1860–83.

R.E. Prothero, *The Psalms in Human Life*, London: J. Murray, 1904.

S.H. Russell, 'Calvin and the Messianic Interpretation of the Psalms', *Scottish Journal of Theology* 21 (1968), 37-47.

H. Schmidt, *Luther und das Buch der Psalmen*, Tübingen: Mohr, 1933.

INDEXES

INDEX OF BIBLICAL REFERENCES

INDEX OF AUTHORS